NUCLEAR WAR: WHAT'S IN IT FOR YOU?

Recent public opinion polls show that Americans are becoming increasingly concerned about the possibility of nuclear war. Ground Zero is a nonpartisan educational organization dedicated to supplying information that the public has a right to know:

How might a nuclear war start?
What would be the consequences of a nuclear war?
How can a nuclear war be prevented?

Ground Zero, headquartered in Washington, D.C., is headed by Roger Molander, for seven years a member of the National Security Council spanning the administrations of presidents Nixon, Ford and Carter. His principal area of responsibility was strategic nuclear policy issues, which included chairing a group which prepared all of the analytical material for the SALT negotiations.

NUCLEAR WAR: WHAT'S IN IT FOR YOU?

GROUND ZERO

PUBLISHED BY POCKET BOOKS NEW YORK

Another *Original* publication of POCKET BOOKS

POCKET BOOKS, a Simon & Schuster division of
GULF & WESTERN CORPORATION
1230 Avenue of the Americas, New York, N.Y. 10020

ISBN: 0-671-45096-4

First Pocket Books printing April, 1982

10 9 8 7 6 5 4

POCKET and colophon are trademarks of Simon & Schuster.

Printed in the U.S.A.

FOR OUR GRANDCHILDREN

CONTENTS

PART II
The Bomb That's Coming to Dinner

PART III
More than You'll Ever Want to Know: The Consequences of Nuclear War

PART IV
Defusing the Bomb

Foreword

The threat that the Soviet Union and the United States might launch nuclear weapons against each other as part of a nuclear war is a reality which confronts us all every day. As we think about this threat we tend to focus either on the *Soviet Union* part or the *nuclear weapons* and *nuclear war* part. We are urged toward these differing perspectives by two interest groups—a "stronger defense" group, which says, "Build more"; and an "arms control" group, which says, "Build less," as a solution to the threat.

We read and listen to the arguments from both sides on such issues as the strategic balance, SALT I and SALT II, B-1 bombers and M-X missiles, the Soviet threat, and necessary or unnecessary increases in defense budgets. The arguments often seem equally reasonable, or equally obscure. In our confusion and frustration as we try to come to grips with the threat of nuclear war, it's natural to want to tune out both groups—as well as the whole subject of nuclear war.

Ground Zero

The Ground Zero organization was created in direct response to the confusion and frustration the American people experience as they confront the threat to their security presented by *the possibility that the Soviet Union and the United States might launch nuclear weapons against each other as part of a nuclear war*. Ground Zero has developed a nonpartisan educational program which will be presented as a part of Ground Zero Week, a nationwide week of community-based discussions and educational events during April 18–25, 1982.

Nuclear War: What's in It for You? was conceived and written as the primary educational resource for the activities of Ground Zero Week. It is also for any individual interested in developing an informed perspective on the threat of nuclear war. Particular effort has been made by Ground Zero to ensure: (1) the presentation of basic, factual information to answer technical questions; and (2) a balanced representation of both sides of policy questions subject to varying analysis and interpretation, especially those questions that draw the primary differences between the "build more" and "build less" perspectives. Ground Zero does not advocate positions on policy questions, nor do any of its educational materials.

As you read *Nuclear War: What's in It for You?* and seek answers to the question posed by the title, you will not always find it pleasant going. While we have done our best to present the material in a light and even entertaining fashion, there's only so much you can do with a grim subject like nuclear war. We wish it were otherwise.

Should you become bogged down in the technical substance or turned off by some of the horrible scenarios described in the book, you may be tempted to put it away, to go back to your everyday life and simply hope or pray that nuclear war never happens. This is a natural reaction, but try to resist the temptation. Unfortunately, there is simply no substitute for confronting the reality of nuclear war if we are to keep it from happening.

We would like to express particular gratitude to the many individuals who made contributions to the preparation of *Nuclear War: What's in It for You?* First, we wish to express our appreciation to David Kenney, Amy Kellem, Jeff Lincoln, Pam Burns, and Vera Steiner, each of whom wrote the initial drafts of chapters of the book, and to Carole Jacobs who did a superb job in editing a difficult manuscript. Bethany Harmon typed the entire manuscript many times over and far more flawlessly than it was written. Finally, Tom Powers deserves special recognition for turning our rough manuscript into its final form.

ROGER C. MOLANDER
Executive Director

EARL A. MOLANDER
Deputy Director

GROUND ZERO

January 5, 1982

PROLOGUE

This Story Will Not Be Reported on Your Evening News

The situation in Teheran on the morning of April 26 was tense. A week earlier the Ayatollah Khomeini had been assassinated by leftist fanatics. During his funeral and in the days that followed, his Islamic fundamentalist followers had filled the streets of Teheran in an emotional display exceeding even that which had accompanied the ousting of the shah.

Now, on April 26, various leftist organizations, which had carefully avoided any challenge to the Islamic fundamentalists over the previous week, took to the streets with a massive rally of their own. Their assessment that the fundamentalists had spent their energy in the emotional response to the ayatollah's death proved in error. By late afternoon bitter street fighting had broken out between the two groups, and by nightfall ten people were reported dead. For the next three days, Iran teetered on the brink of civil war as leftist-fundamentalist clashes spread throughout the country.

The situation became more ominous on April 29, when Iraq, taking advantage of the internal Iranian turmoil, invaded Iran at several points along their common border, just as it had in 1980. By May 8 Iraqi forces had overpowered Iranian defensive forces and succeeded in their objective of capturing the oil fields

1

and the refineries in the Khuzistan region of southwestern Iran.

In Teheran, the leftists and the fundamentalists
blamed each other for the loss of the oil fields, and
fierce fighting erupted in the capital and in several
other major Iranian cities. By May 11 over five hundred people had died in these clashes, and it was
increasingly apparent that the fundamentalist government would soon fall. The Iranian military, which until
now had stayed clear of the internal conflict, made an
unsuccessful effort to seize control of the government.
As fighting between army units and civilians raged
most of the remaining leaders of the Khomeini regime
were killed in a series of terrorist bombing attacks.
What was left of the government collapsed, and
"power lay in the streets."

On May 16 Teheran radio and external communications were seized by a coalition of leftists, including
the Communist Tudeh party and a faction of Islamic
Marxists. Broadcasts claimed that the new group was
the rightful inheritor of Khomeini's Islamic mantle and
that both the Iraqi invasion and the domestic turmoil
were being orchestrated by the "Great Satan"—the
United States of America.

The events that followed had clearly been planned in
advance. The Soviet Union promptly recognized the
new government, calling for withdrawal of Iraqi forces
and offering "advisers" to the new Iranian leadership.
The Iranians quickly accepted the Soviet offer, and
several planeloads of Soviet military and civilian advisers and communications equipment arrived in Teheran on May 17. The Soviet news agency TASS and
other Soviet organs blamed the situation on the CIA,
and the Soviet Union pledged to help restore order in
Iran in the name of "peace-loving peoples everywhere." By the morning of May 18 the Soviet presence had swollen to about fifteen hundred men, with
indications of more to come.

In Washington, the secretary of state issued an immediate public warning that a Soviet military presence in Iran was "unacceptable" to the United States. At the same time the president secretly ordered the U.S. Navy carrier task force in the Indian Ocean and the U.S. Army's 101st and 82nd airborne divisions, the vanguard of the Rapid Deployment Force, to prepare for possible military action in Iran. At a UN Security Council meeting the next day, the ambassadors of Iran and the Soviet Union accused the United States of interfering in the internal affairs of Iran. The Iraqi ambassador heaped abuse on all sides.

On May 22 two divisions of Soviet troops crossed the Soviet-Iranian border "at Iranian request" and began to proceed south. The United States immediately protested to the Soviets that this force of over twelve thousand troops was far larger than was needed for a simple peacekeeping mission.

The Soviet Union disdainfully rejected the American protest.

The United States responded on May 24 by landing a contingent of marines and airborne troops in southwestern Iran. U.S. carrier-based aircraft quickly established air superiority in the region, and within four days the American troops had captured the Khuzistan oil fields and refineries and set up a defensive perimeter around the area. Iraqi forces abandoned the battle.

As the American and Soviet ambassadors traded bitter denunciations at a UN Security Council meeting on May 28 it became clear that neither side was prepared to accept a UN cease-fire in the rapidly escalating conflict. Meanwhile, the numerically superior Soviet force which had entered Iran on May 22 continued to move south toward the oil fields with the announced intention of joining token Iranian troops in the region to push the American forces from Iranian soil. At the same time, U.S. intelligence agencies confirmed preparations for the movement of additional Soviet troops southward from garrisons in the Transcaucasus region of the Soviet Union bordering northeastern Iran.

The Egyptian government offered use of its air bases to the United States, and Israel promptly followed suit. Ignoring Saudi Arabia's demand for high-level consultations before its bases could be used or U.S. planes could cross Saudi airspace, the U.S. government immediately began an all-out effort to resupply and reinforce its troops in Iran. It quickly became apparent, however, that the United States would be unable to move forces into the area fast enough to repulse a committed Soviet assault.

On June 1 the president of the United States, citing the extreme danger to both sides should the crisis continue to escalate, secretly proposed to the Kremlin that the opposing forces enter into an immediate cease-fire in the region and begin negotiations on Persian Gulf security issues. The offer was flatly refused by the Soviets, who called instead for a surrender of the American troops in Iran. The threat of "dire consequences" contained in the president's letter—which could only mean one thing—was ignored.

On June 2 the president convened a meeting of the National Security Council. Faced with the almost certain loss of both U.S. troops and the southwestern Iranian oil fields, the president decided to use nuclear weapons in an effort to stop the Soviet advance. On the morning of June 3 U.S. carrier-based fighter-bombers flew up the Persian Gulf, across Iran, and dropped a dozen nuclear weapons on the supply routes being used by the Soviets in northeastern Iran. The president again called for a cease-fire, but a special late-night session of the UN Security Council on June 3 ended in a shouting match as U.S. and Soviet representatives blamed each other for the first use of nuclear weapons since Hiroshima and Nagasaki.

At dawn on June 5 Soviet Backfire bombers armed with nuclear weapons attacked and destroyed U.S.

forces in southwestern Iran. At the same time the Soviets also attacked the U.S. fleet in the Arabian Sea with Backfires, nuclear-armed torpedoes, and nuclear-armed cruise missiles from submarines. Although most of the Backfires were lost to U.S. carrier-based aircraft, all of the ships in the U.S. Indian Ocean task force were destroyed. In all, the Soviet attack took the lives of nearly ten thousand American soldiers and sailors. There were, essentially, no survivors.

Public debate in the United States over the losses and the crisis bordered on hysteria. Some blamed the United States for the first use of nuclear weapons, but most blamed the Soviet Union and demanded revenge for the lost American lives. The president appealed to the nation for calm and through diplomatic channels demanded immediate Soviet withdrawal from Iran, threatening the further use of nuclear weapons in the region. At the same time he raised the alert status of U.S. nuclear forces, having three days earlier sent all available U.S. missile-carrying submarines to sea and dispersed U.S. bombers to auxiliary airfields.

On June 7 the Soviet Union rejected the U.S. demands and that evening began the evacuation of non-essential personnel from major Soviet cities.

News of the ongoing Soviet evacuation was broadcast on U.S. radio and television networks early that evening. Within a few hours spontaneous evacuation of U.S. cities had begun. In the early-morning hours of June 8 the president, his family and principal advisers, and other key government officials left Washington for undisclosed locations. When the news of these departures leaked out that morning, frantic buying of food and medical supplies immediately ensued. By late on June 8 police and national guardsmen were protecting supermarkets and food-distribution centers and monitoring what had become essentially a panic evacuation of U.S. cities.

On the morning of June 9 the president was advised that Soviet submarines equipped with ballistic missiles were approaching the United States in the Atlantic and Pacific. The navy and especially the air force, alarmed at the growing threat to U.S. bomber bases, recommended military action. The president agreed and authorized the destruction of all Soviet submarines within a thousand miles of the United States, with use of nuclear weapons if necessary. At the same time he informed the Soviet Union of his orders and again demanded that the Soviets take steps to scale down the crisis. Within hours he was notified of the sinking of six Soviet ballistic missile submarines—four of them destroyed by nuclear-tipped torpedoes.

On June 10, ignoring the U.S. warning, the Soviet Union launched a missile attack against ICBM and strategic-bomber bases in the United States. At the same time Moscow passed a message through the still operating Soviet embassy in Washington saying that any retaliatory attack on the Soviet Union by surviving U.S. forces would lead to all-out response against U.S. cities.

When word of the Soviet attack and the Soviet message reached the president, he ordered that no retaliatory action be taken until damage to the United States could be determined. Within an hour he was informed that nearly ten million Americans had been killed instantly by the Soviet attack and that an additional five million people were likely to die from injuries and fallout. All at-sea submarines, 20 percent of the U.S. ICBM force, and 150 American bombers— now in the air and heading for the Soviet Union—had survived. With this information in hand, the president ordered a retaliatory attack against the remaining Soviet land-based missile forces, bomber bases, communications facilities, and other military targets, including Soviet troops stationed along the Soviet-Chinese border. All of the U.S. ICBMs, a quarter of the thirty surviving ballistic missile submarines, and fifty bombers were committed to the attack. The remaining bombers were ordered to return to surviving civilian airfields in the United States.

At the same time the president sent a long personal message to the Soviet president, offering a cease-fire and detailing the consequences for both countries and the world if the war was not halted.

On June 12 the cease-fire was accepted by the Soviets.

On June 13 . . .

In the early evening of June 10, Mike sat in the basement recreation room of his mother's suburban ranch-style home, staring at the television set. The only light in the room, which came from the small ground-level window above him, was fading quickly. Mike tossed a baseball into his glove over and over and over again, stopping periodically to poke at a bowl of cereal on the table beside him.

The television set didn't work. There was no electricity. He shivered, in part from the chill in the damp basement, in part from fear, and in part from the burning sensation on his arms and back. He went over to turn on the furnace. Nothing happened. Then he remembered that even a gas furnace needed electricity to work.

He knew it was past his bedtime, but he couldn't sleep. The strange quiet everywhere was scary, and his arms and back hurt. He felt like crying but was afraid to. Besides, his sister—who was in the next room with his mother—was in far greater pain than he was.

That morning had been weird. His mother, a public-health nurse, had left for work just as he and his sister, Rachel, were getting up, and they had had to prepare their own breakfast. When she said goodbye his mother had hugged them very tightly and told them that if anything happened they should try to get back home as quickly as possible. As he was eating his toast Mike had noticed the headline *Russ Attack on U.S. Unlikely* in the newspaper his mother had left on the kitchen table. He read the first two paragraphs and then turned to the sports section to check on the previous night's baseball scores.

Everything had been weird in school that morning, too. Nobody did their regular work. During math they had talked about missiles and atomic bombs instead of math. In history his teacher had helped Mike and his classmates follow the events of the past two months, first in the Persian Gulf, then in the conflict between the United States and the Soviet Union. At first no one in the class even knew where the Persian Gulf was, and some couldn't say for sure where Russia was, either. They all knew now. They also knew that a week earlier the United States had dropped some kind of little atomic bombs on Russian soldiers who were going after American soldiers near some oil wells in Iran, and then the Russians had used their bombs to kill the American soldiers and sink a lot of American ships. It was all pretty confusing.

By late morning, the teachers seemed to be less worried, kids started talking about the upcoming last day of school, and things almost got back to normal. At lunch Mike poked at his food, the usual junk in the school cafeteria. He took his orange and went out onto the playground.

It was a warm day, and some guys were playing basketball. He joined in. After a few minutes he got hot and took off his shirt. He heard the bell ring and had just grabbed the ball for one last shot when it happened—a sudden, brilliant white flash that illuminated the playground like a thousand giant flashbulbs. For a split second the students in the playground stood as though frozen, riveted by the giant white ball that had appeared just above the horizon to the west. It was as if everyone knew what the white ball was but no one knew what to do. Frightened by the blinding light, Mike quickly turned away and pressed the heels of his hands onto his eyes. Other students stood staring at the white ball and the billowing mushroom cloud that was growing above it.

Mike thought immediately of the shock wave he had been taught would follow quickly. As other students ran for the school building or toward their homes he threw himself down on his stomach in the open playground and covered his head. When the thunderclap came it was deafening, and he felt the enormous pressure, as if ten other kids were on his back. Even when it passed he was afraid to get up, because there was suddenly a wind making a terrible roar. As the wind died down he began to hear other noises—things crashing down and kids screaming.

When Mike at last raised his head, the first thing he saw was that three big trees at the edge of the playground had blown over, and one large branch had fallen within a few yards of his head. As he stood up he could see that at least half of the houses in the development just beyond the schoolyard were flattened or had caved-in roofs. When he turned around he saw the worst thing he had ever seen in his life. The school building had collapsed. Kids were crawling out of piles of bricks and pieces of tangled metal. Some were lying still in the rubble. There was a lot of blood.

Mike stood staring, unbelieving, unsure what to do. There were so many kids hurt, and no adults were in sight. Terrified, he turned around and started to run across the playground toward the development and his house beyond.

As he ran through the streets people began to come out of their houses, some with injuries like the children at school. One man grabbed his arm to stop him and asked what had happened. Although he thought it was the Russians bombing his town, Mike was too afraid to use the words, so he broke free of the man's grasp and ran on.

As he ran up the walk to his house he was relieved to see it still standing, although half the roof was missing and all the windows were blown into the house. He stopped for a moment, then walked slowly up to the large opening that had been the front window and peered in. There was glass all over the floor, and jagged pieces were stuck like knives in the walls. As he turned to climb over the rosebushes to the front door a large piece of glass fell out of the wall and crashed to the floor. He jumped at the sound and for a moment wondered whether he would be safe inside.

Mike dug the key to the front door from his pants pocket and entered the house. He couldn't decide what to do at first. The house looked like it was hit by a tornado. Catching his breath, he walked down the hallway and into the kitchen. The glass was all over. When he opened the door to the basement and flipped the light switch, nothing happened.

He had come home as his mother had told him to, but he wasn't quite sure what he should do next. Even with part of the roof gone and the glass everywhere, it felt better to be in his own home, and the pounding in his head had gone away, although his back had started to feel sort of sunburned. He wondered when his mother would get home and whether his sister's school was as much a disaster as his own. He shut his eyes and prayed that they were both all right.

Mike decided to clean up the glass while he was waiting for his mother. He got a broom and a large wastebasket and went to his room, picking up as much glass as he could and sweeping the rest into a corner. He put all of his books, model airplanes, and sports equipment in their place and straightened things up as he was sure his mother would want him to do. Then he lay down on his bed and tried to read an old comic book.

Mike was awakened by a commotion in the front hallway. He ran out to see his mother and a man he didn't recognize, who was carrying his sister in a blanket. His sister looked terrible. One eye was swollen shut, and she'd been crying a lot. But worse, her right leg was tied to two pieces of scrap lumber and there was a huge, discolored swelling above her knee.

"Rachel's leg's broken," his mother said. "We found her at the school and brought her to the hospital, but there are hundreds of people there hurt much worse than she is, so we brought her home.

"You must get into the basement," his mother went on. "The radiation level from the fallout will soon be very high." Mike wasn't altogether sure what she meant, but he went, anyway. The stranger carried Rachel down the stairs and laid her on the bed in the basement guest room. He said he had better get going, so they all thanked the man, and he left.

Three hours later it was early evening. For dinner they had had cold cereal, what milk had remained in their refrigerator, and ice cream. Rachel was in a lot of pain, and his mother spent most of her time comforting her. She occasionally stopped to give Mike a hug and assure him that everything would be all right, but she looked worried, and once he thought he heard her crying.

Unthinkingly, Mike got up from his chair to turn on the television set to the evening news his mother always watched. He turned the knob, but there was no picture or sound. So he sat down and started throwing the baseball again, waiting for his mother to come and tell him what was going to happen to them.

Later that evening, Sarah Martin sat at an old table in the basement. She was physically exhausted and drained from having tried, however lamely, to reassure Mike about the immediate future. She thought about Mike, about Rachel, about the events of the day. She wondered about her own parents, Mike and Rachel's grandparents. Were they still alive? And her sister, Jennie, the kids' favorite aunt. Where was she? Alive? Dead? With her family? Sarah started to wonder whether she would ever see any of them again. A peculiar emptiness crept over her.

She remembered what it had been like earlier at the

hospital—especially the screams. She had never heard screams like that before—not even from the worst accidents. She thought of all the children—blinded, burned, bleeding, dying. And when they brought in Megan, her friend Karen's little girl . . . well, no use thinking about that anymore. Fortunately for Megan, the hospital still had drugs for the pain. But what would happen when they ran out? She tried not to think about what it would be like for Megan when that happened . . . if she were still alive. What could anyone do? Nothing—that was for sure. They were still bringing people in when Sarah left the hospital with Rachel. But things had become so chaotic that there was little she could have done for anyone had she stayed. There weren't enough medicines or enough doctors. She remembered the anguish in the faces of her colleagues when the order was passed around to stop treating those who obviously wouldn't survive in favor of those who had a chance of being saved.

Suddenly, Sarah recalled a poster she often walked by at the hospital: TODAY IS THE FIRST DAY OF THE REST OF YOUR LIFE. If this is the first day of the rest of my life, she thought, I don't know . . . I just don't know. She stopped herself abruptly. I can't let myself think like this. I'll just have to take it one day at a time, maybe even one hour at a time. Not very reassuring, but Mike and Rachel were alive. Thank God for that. So many people in agony, so many people dead . . .

As though to block out the horror of the day, her mind drifted back in time, to a tragedy she had already accepted. It was two years ago, yet it didn't seem that long. She remembered opening the front door and seeing the two army officers standing there in their crisp and starched uniforms. She knew it was bad news. She had been expecting a call from her husband, Bill, and she realized in an instant that these two men had come to tell her that she would never see him again. They sat in the living room, and the officers explained that Bill had been on a special mission—they called it a national-security mission. She really hadn't listened very carefully or asked many questions. Not that they would have answered them, anyway. It didn't matter. She had just wanted them to leave. She remembered that all the time they were there she was wondering how to tell Rachel and Mike—how to explain why their father was dead. What does national security mean to children, anyway?

She shifted in the chair and thought about Bill's funeral. All those honors. Bill had died "in the interest of national security," but no one seemed to really care. What about *her* security? What about Mike and Rachel's security? Quickly she forced herself to think about something else. She should have known something like this would happen. She remembered the headlines—could it have been only going on for a couple of months? *Ayatollah Khomeini Assassinated. Russians to Police Iran. President Warns Soviets. U.S. Launches Limited Nuclear Strike.* Every week it was something. But they never said there would be a nuclear war. It just seemed so remote, so "out there."

All that careful talk about nuclear weapons. BOMBS, that's what they were really talking about. BOMBS. *Weapons* was just a nice word . . . like when they used to call them devices. That's what they called them after Hiroshima. Bill used to laugh at that—calling a nuclear BOMB a device. It was as if they were trying to somehow disguise what it was—what it meant, what it could do.

It was all so abstract, so remote. People simply don't have nuclear wars. Things could never get so out of control. She tried to recall what she had read in the newspapers about nuclear war. All she could remember were the strange names and numbers. A lot of information about the Russians, about more countries with nuclear weapons, about demonstrations in Europe. Should she have read more carefully? Should she have *tried* to understand all the strange names—M-X, B-1, ICBM, SS-18, MIRV, Backfire, Trident? Well, at this point, it didn't seem to matter very much.

She made herself get up to clear the dishes from the table. How many days can Mike and Rachel eat cold cereal? she wondered. And then where will we get food? As she carried the dishes to the sink in the basement bathroom she realized that there was nothing she could do with them. No water, no electricity, no gas, no phone. No anything. Just silence.

She could hear Rachel softly crying in her sleep in the next room. Mike was curled up asleep in front of the television. If there had been an evening news broadcast, what would it have been like?

She sat down again in the chair and began to play absently with some sugar that had spilled on the table during dinner. Her mind wandered back to a PTA meeting. Someone talking about the possibility of a nuclear war. She couldn't remember who—maybe a neighbor. She remembered wondering at the time what whoever it was thought the PTA could do about a nuclear war. As she sat there in the cold basement the memory became clearer. It had been Mr. Collings from over on Lincoln Avenue. He had argued that the PTA was an important part of the community and that they should do something beyond planning Christmas bazaars and bake sales or choosing new playground equipment. He said he was worried about the possibility of nuclear war. He had talked about his kids and the other kids at school and said we owed it to them to do something. She remembered him saying, "We *can* do something—and God help us if we don't!" She remembered just sitting there, wishing he would go away. It reminded her of Bill and all that national-security talk when he died.

The letter she had received shortly after her husband's death had said Bill had died so we would all be safe. She remembered politicians saying that we needed more weapons to be safe—because the Russians had more weapons. Great. Bill had died and the government had built more weapons, and look at us now. What had happened to all that safety? Who wanted this war? Did the Russians want this war? Did the Russian mothers want this war? She tried to be angry with the Russians—but couldn't. It just didn't seem like a time for anger.

She recalled reading somewhere that the United States had ten thousand nuclear weapons. Ten thousand BOMBS. Had they made her feel safe—safer? She couldn't remember thinking about it at all. She'd left it up to the experts. They said ten thousand weren't enough and they wanted more—for national security, of course. She suddenly felt bitter. Mike and Rachel and the other children who survived this wouldn't inherit the earth, they'd inherit "devices," "weapons," bombs and more bombs.

I should have done something then, she thought. I should have done something before this happened. I should have taken the time to think about it, but there were bake sales and playground equipment, and my nurses' meeting . . . and it was too terrifying to think about. How could I be expected to contemplate the death of my children? But at least I should have admitted that it scared me, that I was frightened and confused. I should have told someone. . . .

She got up and walked over to where Mike was sleeping, intending to wake him up and put him to bed on the couch. But as she watched him sleeping peacefully she decided to let him be. Better he should sleep. She went to check on Rachel in the other room. Poor Rachel, she thought, she never hurt anyone. Her leg must hurt terribly, and she's one of the lucky ones. Lucky to be alive. Lucky to be alive . . ."

She gently sat down next to Rachel on the cot and

began stroking her hair. *Could* I have done something? she wondered. Could I have kept this from happening? Maybe if I had told them that ten thousand nuclear weapons didn't really make me feel safe. Maybe if a lot of people had spoken up, had cared a little more . . . it would have made a difference.

She looked at her watch. It had stopped, too. It didn't seem to matter. It was dark, and there was tomorrow to face.

PART I

The Bomb in Your Backyard

1

From Toyland to Never-Never Land: The Story of the First Atomic Bomb

It was fear that built the atomic bomb—fear that Hitler would get it first and use it to conquer the world. But before the fear came the thrill of scientific discovery, and, in spite of its tragic potential, the story of the atomic bomb has the best features of a dozen contemporary mystery and spy novels packed into a single, high-intensity drama. It has a set of eccentric characters—most of them scientists and many of them geniuses—including Albert Einstein and other refugees from Nazi tyranny. It has challenging mysteries: first the secret of the structure of the atom, and then the riddle of the elusive "chain reaction" recognized early as the key to making an atomic bomb. There are contraband goods, "heavy water" and "yellow cake" uranium ore that might have enabled the Nazis to build an atomic bomb, spirited out of Western Europe in the midst of war. There is a frantic race against time. And there is a heroine, an Austrian scientist who smuggles out the first clue to the elusive "chain reaction." The story has everything except a happy ending.

It all started innocently enough . . .

Einstein, Merlin, and Other Alchemists

Albert Einstein—whose genius was yet to be discovered—appears in the opening scene. It is Europe, just before World War I, and he is lecturing at a university. On the blackboard behind him is "E = mc^2," a mathematical equation that will ultimately become almost as well known as "2 + 2 = 4" in a world which only barely comprehends its meaning. Einstein is awkward and disheveled, a young physicist who could not find a job when he first graduated from college. And he has a new theory.

In German (for Einstein is a German Jew) he explains that according to his "theory of relativity," matter is simply "frozen energy." He has expressed the relationship between matter and this frozen energy by the simple equation on the blackboard: "E" is energy, "m" is mass or weight, and "c" is the speed of light. He points out, perhaps with a sly wink, that if a piece of matter could actually be *converted* to its "frozen energy," the amount of energy released would be enormous. The speed of light, he reminds his students, is 186,000 miles *per second*. The total conversion of only one *ounce* of matter to its "frozen energy" would be equivalent to the explosion of a million tons of TNT.

Einstein's colleagues are impressed by his mathematics and his lucidity, but they recognize that the conversion of matter to energy is preposterous. It would be easier for them to believe in Merlin's magic or in medieval alchemists converting lead to gold. Einstein's proposition was just another interesting scientific theory and—as so frequently happened—it would soon be disproved. Or would it?

Copernicus and a Melancholy Dane

Enter a Danish physicist. It is the early 1920s. Four centuries earlier, another Dane, named Copernicus, had stood the scientific and religious community on its ear by arguing that the earth and the other planets revolved around the sun. The modern Dane, Niels Bohr, is explaining that the smallest particle known to man, the atom, is essentially a miniature solar system—a central nucleus (sun) surrounded by orbiting electrons (planets).

This was not the first model of the atom, but it was clear that this was the right model. Just as planets are held in orbit by the force of gravity, the negatively charged electrons were held in their orbits by the electrical force from the positively charged nucleus.

The first mystery, the basic structure of the atom, had been solved.

Meanwhile, on a Misty Island . . .

The scene is now England, where the excitement of the revolution taking place in twentieth-century physics has galvanized a battery of distinguished British physicists. One of them, Ernest Rutherford, played a key role in the work leading to the Bohr model of the atom. At one point, when criticized for his absence from a meeting of a British weapons-research committee during World War I, Rutherford retorted: "Talk softly, please. I have been engaged in experiments which suggest that the atom can be artificially disintegrated. If it is true, it is of far greater importance than a war." But not even Rutherford dreamed how true that statement was.

It is now 1932, and a British physicist named Chadwick, experimenting with radioactive materials, discovers a strange new atomic particle which has *no* electric charge. Chadwick names his new particle the neutron, and physicists quickly start to develop new models of the atom in which the neutron plays a key role. It begins to appear that the structure of the positively charged atomic nucleus itself must be a combination of positively charged particles (called protons) and the newly discovered neutrons. (See Figure 1.1.)

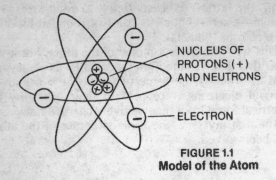

FIGURE 1.1
Model of the Atom

Einstein and the Elusive "Chain Reaction"

It is now 1934, and Einstein is a refugee from Nazi Germany and living in the United States. He is attending a symposium sponsored by the American Association for the Advancement of Science to discuss the possibility of making "nuclear weapons." His theory of relativity is now widely accepted. Further developments in physics have led to speculation about the possibility of making weapons in which some of the "frozen energy" in atomic nuclei would be released. In particular, it has been found that bombarding certain materials with Chadwick's neutrons can make them radioactive, literally "active" in releasing highly energetic subatomic particles and gamma rays. Another refugee from Hitler, Hungarian physicist Leo Szilard, has suggested that a chain of such reactions might be sustained. Einstein expresses serious doubt that such a chain reaction is possible.

Enter the Heroine

It is now the autumn of 1938, and the scene has shifted to Berlin, where Hitler is secretly laying plans for the conquest of Europe. In another part of the city a team of German physicists led by Otto Hahn and Franz Strassman are making a startling experimental discovery. They have been bombarding a mass of uranium with a stream of low-speed neutrons, and it appears that the uranium atoms—or, more precisely, their nuclei—are breaking in two. The breaking of the uranium nuclei is remarkable enough, but in addition it appears that each time a uranium nucleus is split two or three neutrons are released in a reaction that is much like an explosion—that is, all of the four (or sometimes five) pieces from the broken nucleus are moving at extraordinary speeds. (See Figure 1.2.) Some type of highly energetic reaction was clearly taking place in the uranium nucleus.

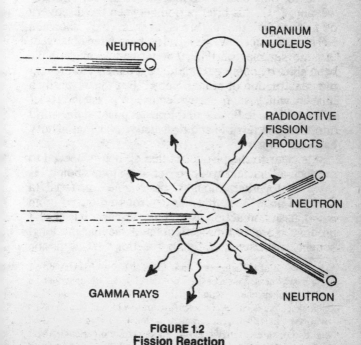

FIGURE 1.2
Fission Reaction

Shortly after this discovery, Lise Meitner, an Austrian member of the German scientific team, flees to Denmark, where she reports the results of the experiment to Niels Bohr. Bohr immediately recognizes the significance of the German discovery, which Meitner has named "fission." He spreads the news to colleagues in the scientific communities of Western Europe and America—communities which include many nuclear physicists who, like Meitner, have fled Nazi tyranny.

The Secret Is Out

A number of scientists quickly recognize that the German discovery of uranium fission signals the potential for the "chain reaction" necessary for "nuclear weapons." Of this brief period between the discovery of fission and the outbreak of war, the renowned German physicist Werner Heisenberg later observed: "In the summer of 1939, twelve people might have been able, by coming to mutual agreement, to prevent the construction of atom bombs." But this is hardly a time in which such an agreement is possible. Hitler will soon invade Poland and France, pushing the world into the most terrible and destructive war that history had ever known.

It is clear to the physicists that all that is needed to produce a "nuclear weapon" or an "atomic bomb" is to bring together enough "fissionable" material (a "critical mass") so that the neutrons produced in an initial fission reaction would not escape but would produce more and more fissions, achieving the long-sought self-sustaining "chain reaction."* One fission

---

*The concept of a chain reaction is familiar to any freeway driver who has witnessed a succession of "tail-enders." To understand a self-sustaining chain reaction, picture a freeway situation where an initial accident is caused by a tire (neutron) which is thrown off an overpass and strikes a car (uranium nucleus). This car splits in half *and* two or three of its wheels fly off and strike other cars. These cars also split in half, and the process repeats. Since each accident (fission) leads to two or three others, it is easy to see how fast the chain reaction would progress.

would create two more, those two additional four, four eight, and so on—all in the blink of an eye. (See Figure 1.3.) The release of so much "frozen energy" in a single instant would constitute a mighty explosion.

Because the Germans were known to understand this phenomenon as well, many American scientists and recent European emigrés worry that Nazi Germany might develop a bomb using the fission process—the most destructive bomb the world has ever seen. The lore of the period is filled with stories of one scientist, Leo Szilard, scurrying around New York telling anyone of influence who will listen about the awful potential of an atomic bomb and the dire consequences if the Nazis are the first to perfect this weapon.

The Spur of Fear

It is now July of 1939. Einstein's theory of relativity has brought him worldwide fame and influence. He is persuaded by Szilard and his fellow scientists to write

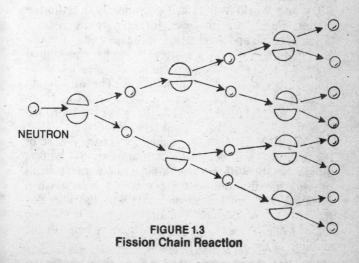

NEUTRON

FIGURE 1.3
Fission Chain Reaction

a letter to President Roosevelt explaining that the fission process discovered by the German scientists has now made a nuclear bomb a practical possibility. Roosevelt is notably unenthusiastic until he is told the story of a similar overture by a young American inventor, Robert Fulton, to Napoleon. Fulton told Napoleon of his scheme to build a fleet of steam-powered vessels that would enable France to invade England. Napoleon dismissed Fulton's idea as preposterous and suffered the judgment of history. Fearful of sharing Napoleon's fate, Roosevelt appoints an Advisory Committee on Uranium to investigate Einstein's claim. The committee agrees with Einstein that fission might be used to start a chain reaction in uranium. A number of chain-reaction experiments follow. In the spring of 1941, a review committee predicts that a chain reaction might be achieved within eighteen months and that a nuclear bomb might be produced within four years. These predictions are to prove uncannily accurate.

The attack on Pearl Harbor and the United States' entry into World War II in December 1941 settle the matter. Funds are provided for both research on a possible bomb and production of the necessary fissionable material. Within a matter of weeks, the United States' nuclear weapons program changes its focus from research to actual production. The Manhattan Engineer District Office of the U.S. Corps of Engineers is formed in May 1942 as the cover for coordination of the supersecret "Manhattan Project."

In June 1942 Robert Oppenheimer is named head of the team that will design the actual weapon—the first atomic bomb. Within six months, a major step toward proving the feasibility of a bomb is achieved when Enrico Fermi, an Italian physicist who has also fled the Nazis, succeeds in creating the first man-made nuclear chain reaction in a squash court beneath the stadium of the University of Chicago.

Inexorable Momentum

The saga of the Manhattan Project is one of the most remarkable stories of human determination and achievement in all of history. Both the name of the project and the name of its director have become synonymous with the atomic bomb and nuclear weapons development. In a matter of months Oppenheimer secretly brought many of the best scientists and technicians in America to a remote site in New Mexico—Los Alamos. It was a massive undertaking— a total work force of thousands which was spending money at the rate of over $1 billion a year by 1944. Oppenheimer, a brilliant physicist of broad-ranging intellectual interests, proved to be a remarkable manager as the project overcame tremendous problems in both physics and engineering. While the bomb development and design program was progressing at Los Alamos, two other hugh engineering projects at Hanford, Washington, and Oak Ridge, Tennessee, were producing the necessary fuel—the fissionable material for the weapons.

Meanwhile, the motivation driving the development of an atomic bomb was undergoing a significant change. The original impetus for the project—the fear that the Germans were also working on nuclear weapons development—remained strong well into 1944. But by that time the project was generating its own energy, and fear was replaced by the desire to have the bomb as a weapon for its own sake.

Nazi Failure

In Germany, the first steps toward building a bomb had been remarkably similar to those in the United States. In April 1939 an Einstein-like letter enthusiastically endorsing nuclear weapons development was sent to the German War Office, which consequently established a special bureau for the military application of nuclear fission. The bureau promoted chain-reaction experiments like the one which Fermi performed at the University of Chicago stadium as well as studies to find ways of producing bomb-grade uranium.

But the Germans' bomb project and its supporters failed to make progress. Some of their difficulties were their own fault, while others were outside their control. Early calculations, eventually shown to be in error, had led to a decision to use "heavy water"—water in which the hydrogen atom, the H in H_2O, has an extra neutron in its nucleus—in the chain-reaction experiments. Heavy water occurs naturally in the ocean but requires considerable time and electrical energy for separation. Almost the entire world supply of heavy water (four hundred pounds) had been spirited out of France just before the German invasion, and Nazi attempts to produce more in Norway were frustrated when an Allied commando team blew up the factory.

The heavy-water decision was the main reason for the failure of the German atomic bomb project, but other factors were also at work. These included the flight of many top scientists from Germany; the inability of the bomb program to compete for money and men with such other German military developments as Wernher Von Braun's V-1 and V-2 rocket program; and the repeated destruction of laboratory facilities by Allied bombing attacks.

Trinity—a Religious Experience

By early 1945 it was clear that the Germans would not have an atomic bomb. Knowing this, some American scientists sought to shut down or delay the Manhattan Project. But the momentum of the project was now being sustained as much by the desire to know whether or not the bomb could be built as by any clear idea of how and why the bomb would be used.

Whatever its motivation, the Manhattan Project ultimately was a success. On July 16, 1945, the first atomic bomb, code-named Trinity, was exploded at Alamagordo, New Mexico, a desolate stretch of desert two hundred miles south of Los Alamos.

Before the test, there was a betting pool among the Los Alamos scientists on what the explosive force of the bomb would be. No Los Alamos scientist guessed higher than five thousand tons of TNT. One visiting scientist, I. I. Rabi, guessed ten thousand tons, just to flatter his hosts.

On the day of the test one of the scientists watching it, Enrico Fermi, conducted a small experiment. He tore up a piece of paper into small bits, and when the bomb went off, began dropping them to the ground. When the shock wave from the explosion fifteen miles away reached the scientists, it blew the bits of paper Fermi was dropping a foot or two. Fermi measured the distance, consulted some figures he had worked out beforehand, and announced the force of the explosion. "Twenty thousand tons," he said.

Like the others, Oppenheimer was stunned by the sheer magnitude of the blast. A passage from Hindu scripture came to his mind as the mushroom cloud rose up toward the heavens: "I am become death, shatterer of worlds."

2

Everything You Ever Wanted to Know about Nuclear Weapons: How They Work and What They Can Do

Nuke Hanoi. Nuke Iran. Nuke Ohio State. Nuke the Whales. Nuke 'em back to the Stone Age. That's the message on bumper stickers and rest-room walls, short and not so sweet. *Nuke* has become just another four-letter word. But suppose you or someone else really did want to build an atomic bomb of your own and nuke somebody. The first atomic bomb took three years and $3 billion. What would it take to make one today?

How to Make an Atomic Bomb

To assemble a working atomic bomb you need three things: (1) knowledge of how a bomb works; (2) a sufficient amount (a "critical mass") of fissionable material such as uranium 235 or plutonium 239; and (3) a means of bringing that fissionable material together in a way that ensures that it will explode only where you want it to, and not in your basement.

In 1939 nobody was sure how to build a nuclear weapon, but today the practical knowledge necessary to make a crude atomic bomb is readily available. The general principles are described in most encyclopedias and high-school physics books. Just look for the article or chapter entitled "Atomic Bomb" or "Nuclear Weapons" or "Fission."

Essentially, what is involved in a nuclear explosion is the bringing together of a "critical mass" of uranium 235 (235 refers to the total number of neutrons and protons in the nucleus of one atom) or plutonium 239 to set in motion the rapid "chain reaction" that precedes a nuclear explosion.

To visualize the creation of a critical mass of fissionable material, imagine yourself with a pile of snow that is really uranium 235 or plutonium 239. If you were to begin packing your fissionable snow into a snowball and stopped at the size of a golf ball, it would be too small; you would still not have the necessary critical mass. Even if the fission process got started, too many neutrons would be escaping from the surface of the snowball to sustain the necessary chain reaction. However, if you were to slowly increase your snowball to the size of a baseball, you would have reached a critical mass. If you started the fission process inside your snowball, there would be more neutrons produced than could escape from the surface.* Remember, it is the neutrons that split other U-235 or P-239 atoms, which in turn split still *other* atoms, and so on. A critical mass becomes "critical" at the point where it can't safely get rid of its neutrons.

Having reached critical mass, you now have one millionth of a second to throw your snowball at someone you don't like, because that's how long it takes for a critical mass of fissionable material to create a nuclear explosion. In this period, 2,000,000, 000,000,000,000,000,000 atoms of uranium or plutonium split apart, or "fission." The resulting atomic fragments—new smaller atoms, neutrons, and gamma

---

*This phenomenon is explained by the fact that the volume of a sphere and the total number of atoms in the sphere are proportional to the radius cubed, whereas the surface area and the number of surface atoms from which a neutron can escape is a function of the radius squared.

radiation (similar to X rays)—shoot about at high speed, causing your snowball to reach temperatures so high (10,000,000°F.—much hotter than the surface of the sun) that the ball cannot stay together and an explosion results.

The technical details of atomic bomb design and the triggering of an atomic explosion are actually a bit more complicated than packing a snowball of fissionable material into a critical mass, but not much. The secret is to pack the snowball quickly when you want it to go off. The really hard part of building a bomb is the collection of the necessary amount of fissionable material.

Uranium occurs in nature, but not very plentifully. The United States today gets its uranium from Utah and Canada; the Soviet Union gets its uranium from Czechoslovakia. Uranium is also mined in Zaire, Australia, and elsewhere. Finding uranium ore is difficult, but separating the element from its ore is even more difficult. Even harder than that is separating radioactive uranium 235 from uranium 238, since the latter makes up 99.3 percent of naturally occurring uranium. Plutonium presents an even greater problem, since it does not occur naturally at all but must be created by bombarding uranium 238 with neutrons.* During World War II, the U.S. government plant at Oak Ridge was the source of the uranium 235 used for the Manhattan Project. The plutonium used in the Manhattan Project was made in nuclear reactors at Hanford, Washington. Producing fissionable material was a huge industrial undertaking of an entirely new sort, so large and so new some experts thought it would take Russia twenty years to match the feat. In fact, it took four.

Assuming you have collected, bought, or stolen the necessary amount of fissionable material to make a

---

*When a uranium 238 nucleus absorbs a neutron, it becomes uranium 239, which is radioactive. The uranium 239 decays in a process which eventually produces plutonium 239.

bomb, the next trick is to time the final packing of your destructive snowball so that it explodes somewhere other than in your own hands.

The Manhattan Project used two methods. The Hiroshima bomb, made of uranium 235, used a gun-type method. A conventional explosive at one end of the bomb fired a half snowball or more of U-235 at another half snowball of U-235 at the other end. The two formed a critical mass when they met and were held together for the necessary one millionth of a second. The resulting explosion is now in the history books.

The first atomic bomb test at Alamagordo, New Mexico, and the Nagasaki bomb were of the implosion type. (See Figure 2.1.) A hollow sphere of plutonium was surrounded by a second sphere of conventional (TNT) explosive. The entire outer sphere was ignited

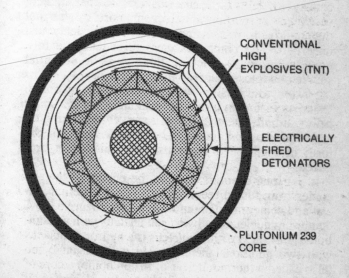

CONVENTIONAL
HIGH
EXPLOSIVES (TNT)

ELECTRICALLY
FIRED
DETONATORS

PLUTONIUM 239
CORE

FIGURE 2.1
Atomic (Fission) Bomb

by an electrical charge which blasted inward from all sides at once, thus compressing the plutonium into a critical mass. Because plutonium produces neutrons less efficiently than does uranium 235, an independent neutron source—called an initiator or "urchin"—was used to trigger the nuclear explosion. The implosion principle is now the method used for most bombs. It offers the greatest efficiency in use of fissionable material and the greatest flexibility.

How to Make a Hydrogen (Thermonuclear) Bomb

After World War II, researchers seeking to increase the destructive power of atomic weapons found that increasing the size of fission bombs—trying to make a bigger critical mass—made them too heavy and clumsy to deliver. There was talk at that time of sneaking monster bombs into enemy ports by ship, but that approach was dismissed as too unwieldy and uncertain. The bomb designers turned instead to a new technology—nuclear fusion—as a potential source of explosive energy for bigger bangs.

Fission and fusion work in opposite manners. Whereas fission involves the breaking apart of a single heavy atomic nucleus, fusion involves the fusing together of two light nuclei. In both cases, energy in the form of high-speed neutrons and radiation is produced.

It has long been known that the energy of the sun comes from fusion reactions involving deuterium nuclei and sometimes tritium nuclei. (See Figure 2.2.) A deuterium nucleus is a hydrogen nucleus with an additional neutron; a tritium nucleus is a hydrogen nucleus with two additional neutrons. In a hydrogen bomb (also called a thermonuclear or fusion bomb) a core of deuterium and tritium is ignited by the explosion of an atomic bomb. The radiation from the atomic bomb explosion is focused on a Styrofoam explosive sur-

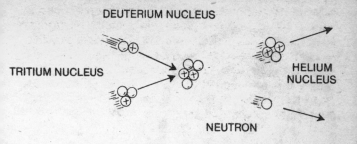

DEUTERIUM NUCLEUS

TRITIUM NUCLEUS

HELIUM
NUCLEUS

NEUTRON

FIGURE 2.2
Fusion Reaction

rounding the hydrogen bomb. (See Figure 2.3.) This explosive in turn compresses and raises the temperature of the deuterium-tritium core to about 20,000,000° F., at which point fusion occurs and the bomb explodes.

Most hydrogen bombs also include an outer shell of uranium 238 around the deuterium-tritium core. The highly energetic neutrons that are released in the fusion process are absorbed by the uranium 238, causing its nuclei to fission. Thus, most hydrogen bombs are fission-fusion-fission devices.

If there is no uranium 238 around the deuterium-tritium core to absorb the neutrons released by the fusion, the neutrons spray outward from the bomb as a deadly form of radiation. This is essentially what happens in a so-called neutron bomb.

Measuring the Size of Bombs

The energy released (called the yield) by a nuclear explosion is commonly measured in tons of TNT. (Don't ask why; no one remembers.)

The yield of early atomic bombs was measured in

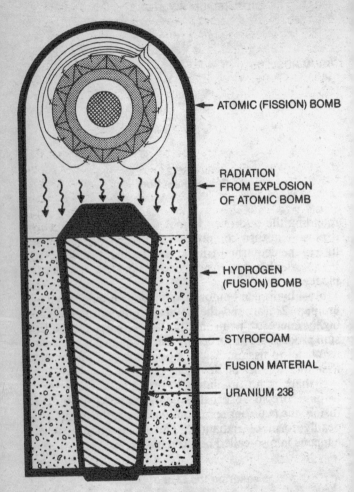

ATOMIC (FISSION) BOMB

RADIATION
FROM EXPLOSION
OF ATOMIC BOMB

HYDROGEN
(FUSION) BOMB

STYROFOAM

FUSION MATERIAL

URANIUM 238

FIGURE 2.3
Hydrogen (Fusion) Bomb

kilotons (thousands of tons) and was in the 20-kiloton range. The Hiroshima bomb had a yield of about 15 kilotons. Some hydrogen bombs in the Soviet arsenal today are over 20 megatons (millions of tons) in size— over a thousand times larger than the Hiroshima bomb. The largest U.S. bomb, tested on March 1, 1954, had a yield of 15 megatons. The largest Soviet bomb, tested in 1961, was approximately 50 megatons.

What a Well-Made Bomb Can Do

Nuclear weapons are bombs, and nothing about the effects of bombs makes pleasant reading. This is especially true of nuclear weapons, which are not only much more powerful than ordinary bombs but also produce X rays, gamma rays, fallout, and other new and insidious effects that poison or otherwise damage the human body. Thus the reader can be excused for skimming over the material that follows and going on to Chapter 3.

The immediate or "prompt" effects of nuclear weapons can be separated into three categories, corresponding to the three forms of energy released by the nuclear explosion—blast, heat, and radiation. All three are lethal.

Blast Effects

In a fraction of a second the explosion of an atom bomb creates a powerful blast wave in the form of a wall of compressed air. It is physically the same as the blast wave produced by a conventional bomb, only much more powerful. The blast wave moves away from "ground zero," the point of detonation of a nuclear weapon, at a speed of at least 12.5 miles a minute, or 750 miles per hour, which is slightly faster than the speed of sound. Extensive physical damage results from the "overpressure" of the blast wave— the amount by which the pressure of the blast wave

exceeds normal atmospheric pressure—and from the
high winds (called dynamic pressure) which follow
behind it.

There is considerable variation in the effects of the
blast wave on physical objects. Most buildings will
collapse under about five pounds per square inch of
overpressure. Remarkably, the human body can with-
stand overpressures up to two hundred pounds per
square inch (fourteen times normal atmospheric pressure) before sustaining physiological damage. But
blast effects do kill and injure many people who are
caught in falling structures or hit by flying debris or
glass.

Thermal Effects

The TNT in a conventional bomb produces a temperature of a few thousand degrees. In the central and
hottest region of a nuclear explosion, called the fireball, temperatures reach millions of degrees and enormous amounts of heat (called thermal radiation) are
released. This thermal radiation is the same as the heat
that one feels from a radiator or from standing in front
of a fireplace.

About 35 percent of the energy from an atomic
explosion is in the form of thermal radiation. There are
two thermal radiation pulses from an explosion. The
first occurs as the fireball starts to form and is of short
duration and thus causes few casualties. The second
follows about a second later. Because thermal radiation travels at the speed of light (186,000 miles per
second) it precedes the blast wave, which travels at
the speed of sound, just as lightning precedes thunder.

Thermal radiation injures in two ways—directly in
the form of skin burns, and indirectly by causing fires.
Burns from thermal radiation vary directly with proximity to ground zero and the magnitude of the explosion. The closer you are, the worse the burn. A

one-megaton bomb, the approximate size of many of today's nuclear weapons, would cause fatal burns to people caught in the open within at least a five-mile radius of ground zero. Burns were among the most ghastly injuries caused by the bomb dropped on Hiroshima.

The thermal radiation from a nuclear explosion can also start fires, just as the sun's rays, if concentrated by a magnifying glass, can ignite a leaf or a piece of paper. Additional fires would be started by blast damage to furnaces and electrical systems. Scientists disagree just how widespread such fires would be, however. Massive fires of the kind that followed the San Francisco earthquake (called conflagrations) or fires which result from high winds (called fire storms) will not necessarily occur, but might. For example, there was a fire storm at Hiroshima—as there had been in the conventional bombing of Tokyo—but not at Nagasaki. Fire storms kill not only through heat, but also through asphyxiation of people in shelters. The fire consumes oxygen at such a rapid rate it literally sucks air out of the places where people are hiding.

Radiation Effects

While the initial burst of neutrons and gamma rays would be lethal in the immediate vicinity of the explosion, blast and thermal effects would constitute the major hazards in this region. The principal source of death and energy from radiation would be from radioactive fallout. These effects are discussed in Chapter 10.

Chapter 10 also addresses the effects on society itself, which might collapse under a major nuclear assault. The survivors who get through the first days or weeks might live to regret their "luck" when they found nothing to eat, no heat in winter, no help in rebuilding.

What You Now Know, whether You Wanted to or Not

Whether you were fascinated with the technical details of bomb-making or not, there were two facts about nuclear weapons in this chapter which no doubt captured your attention. First, if you can gain access to fissionable materials, nuclear weapons are relatively easy to make. Most modern nations have the capacity to make them, and you and a carefully selected group of coconspirators could probably make one yourselves.

Second, nuclear weapons destroy in a variety of equally unpleasant but "efficient" ways. The awful effects of blast, fire, and radiation on people and their environment are attractive from a military cost-effectiveness point of view while abhorrent in human terms.

3

Throwing the Bomb:
The Evolution of Nuclear
Weapon Delivery Systems

The history of war is largely the history of weapons and weapons delivery systems. The first weapons—stones, clubs, spears, swords—were either wielded or thrown by the human arm, a remarkably adaptable weapon delivery system. Gradually men found ways to strike farther, more accurately, with greater force. Instead of throwing stones, men learned to hurl them with slings. The throwing spear was replaced by the bow and arrow, the conventional bow by the crossbow—a delivery system of such fearsome power it was condemned by some medieval popes as illicit for use against Christians. The continuing historical quest for weapons with more destructive power, greater accuracy, and faster delivery has led in turn to the catapult, the cannon, the musket, ships of the line, aircraft, and finally the intercontinental ballistic missile.

When the Manhattan Project began, some scientists—including Einstein—thought an atomic bomb would be so big and heavy that it would have to be delivered by ship. (Later, after work had begun in earnest on thermonuclear weapons in the late 1940s, Robert Oppenheimer predicted they would have to be delivered by "ox cart.") But the technicians kept the bomb down to manageable size, and in 1945 the Hiroshima bomb, weighing 9,000 pounds, was delivered by a B-29 bomber with modified bomb-bay doors. The delivery itself was no more complicated than the daily bombing run over Japan.

The thirty-five years since the first atomic bomb was dropped have seen a dramatic revolution in weapons delivery systems. Nuclear weapons can now be delivered not only by long-range bombers but also by missiles fired from underground silos and underwater submarines, by artillery shells fired from mobile cannon, by retreating troops who leave them behind as land mines, and by ships which drop them into the sea as depth charges and torpedoes. The accuracy and speed of delivery for nuclear weapons are now measured in feet and seconds on the battlefield and in hundreds of feet and minutes at intercontinental distances. This revolution has been made possible largely by improvements in the nuclear warheads themselves, which are now smaller in size, lighter in weight, more powerful in yield, and available in greater numbers.

Bombers: The First Delivery System and Still Looking Good

The initial step in the evolution of delivery systems specially designed for nuclear weapons was the B-36 bomber, a huge craft with a 230-foot wingspan and six propeller engines facing to the rear. First deployed by the United States in 1948 but not fully operational until 1951, the B-36 was designed to carry nuclear bombs to a range of up to 4,000 miles. Until then, U.S. nuclear bombs were carried on B-29s modified in much the same manner as the B-29 that dropped the atomic bomb on Hiroshima. The B-36 was followed by the B-47, the first American heavy bomber with jet engines. In-flight refueling allowed these bombers to reach Soviet territory from the United States as well as from bases in Western Europe and the Far East.

In 1955, the first of the truly intercontinental bombers, the B-52, began to be deployed. In the intervening twenty-five years the B-52 has been the backbone of the American intercontinental bomber force. During this period, the air force has often pushed for a modern replacement, but so far none has been built. Instead, the B-52 has been frequently redesigned and retrofitted with new weapons, new electronic equipment, and even new engines. Eight versions of the B-52 have been built, with the last B-52s, the B-52Hs, coming off the production line in 1965. The latest B-52s have a range of about 8,000 miles and a maximum speed of 650 miles per hour, just under the speed of sound. They can fly as low as a few hundred feet off the ground—a very effective tactic for evading enemy radars.

Today's B-52s can carry many different kinds of weapons. For example, a single B-52 can carry as many as eight short-range attack missiles (SRAMs), twelve cruise missiles (range about 2,000 miles), and four bombs—all armed with nuclear warheads. Nevertheless, the B-52 force is growing old and eventually will have to be replaced—although the latest model B-52s (about 160 B-52Gs and 100 B-52Hs) should remain effective delivery systems into the early 1990s.

The advantages of intercontinental bombers are considerable even in an age of missiles. As manned delivery systems with direct communications to military commanders in the continental United States, they can be directed to new targets while in flight or even recalled after launch—an important factor in the event of false alarms. Thus it is not surprising that the search for a replacement for the aging B-52s has occupied the attention of the last five presidential administrations.

The latest decision (and don't bet the rent money or the mortgage payment that it won't change) was announced by President Reagan in September 1981. It calls for the production of one hundred B-1 supersonic bombers, with the first aircraft to be deployed by 1984. This "new B-1" is similar to, but not the same as, the "old B-1" canceled by President Carter. One of the principal reasons Carter canceled the "old B-1" (in addition to cost) was the inability of the aircraft to carry long-range cruise missiles. A major redesign of the aircraft has corrected that shortcoming in the "new B-1."

Even though the B-1 will be able to fly at twice the speed of sound—about 1,500 miles per hour—it will rarely use this option. To save fuel, B-1s will fly at subsonic speeds between the United States and the periphery of the Soviet Union, with a total flight time of six to eight hours to the first launch of a weapon.

Research work is also proceeding on a second advanced bomber, called Stealth because it is hoped that technological advances will make the bomber almost invisible to Soviet radars and other systems for detecting aircraft. The techniques for "decreasing the radar cross section" include coating the airplane with material which absorbs radar signals and changing the shapes of wings, engine inlets, and so forth, so that reflected radar signals are weaker. An effort is also being made to "cool" the new aircraft so it cannot be detected with heat-sensing devices. It is hoped that Stealth technology will permit U.S. bombers to fly over Soviet territory carrying a mix of bombs and short-range missiles well past the end of the century. The alternative is for the bomber force eventually to rely on long-range cruise missiles, which might themselves use Stealth-type technology, launched from outside Soviet territory. We will not know until the late 1980s whether Stealth technology is successful— or whether the Soviets will be able to find some alternative means of detecting such aircraft.

Soviet bomber development was initially similar to that of the United States, but a few years behind. The early Soviet medium-range bombers of the B-29 type could reach the continental United States, but only on one-way missions. In 1954 and 1955, the first truly intercontinental Soviet bombers, called the Bear and the Bison, appeared at the annual Mayday flyby over Red Square in Moscow. This unexpected development led to predictions of a "bomber gap" which would give the Soviet Union nuclear superiority in the late 1950s. The bomber gap never materialized, however, for the Soviets built fewer than two hundred Bisons and Bears, concentrating their efforts instead on ICBMs.

In the late 1970s the Soviets initiated production of a new bomber, the Backfire, intended for missions against Europe, China, and naval targets. By the end of 1981, about three hundred of these aircraft had been produced. Because the Backfire has a substantially greater range than previous Soviet aircraft with the same missions, there has been some speculation that it might be used against targets in the United States, even though only one-way high-altitude missions would be possible. So far, however, there is no evidence that the Soviets intend to use the Backfire in this manner.

There are some indications, including claims by the Soviets themselves, that a new Soviet intercontinental bomber is on the drawing boards. So far about all we know about it is its name—the Tupolev-160.

As implied in the title of this section, bombers are still very popular nuclear weapon delivery systems and are likely to remain so for the foreseeable future. The ability of bombers to be launched on warning and recalled is a particularly attractive characteristic as compared to the hair-trigger nature of the missiles. Speaking of which . . .

Ballistic Missiles: How They Work

If you have ever thrown a baseball (or a rock), you can understand how a ballistic missile works. Think of the missile warhead as the baseball, the missile guidance system as your brain, the missile booster* as your arm, and the warhead release mechanism as your fingers. In both cases there is also of course a target. You are now ready to launch/throw.

The "launch" signal goes from the guidance system to the missile booster in the same way that the "throw" signal goes from your brain to your arm. As the missile booster burns, it moves the warhead along a path to the target at greater and greater speed, just as your arm directs and propels the baseball. When the guidance system senses that the missile warhead is going fast enough to fly unaided to the target, it shuts off the rocket engines in the booster and instructs the warhead release mechanism to release the warhead. Similarly, when the baseball is moving at the proper speed and in the right direction to reach its intended target, your brain instructs your fingers to release the baseball. For the balance of their flights both the missile warhead and the baseball are essentially traveling on what is called a ballistic trajectory, meaning only the force of gravity (plus a little air resistance in the case of the baseball) is acting on them—thus the name ballistic missile.

Figure 3.1 depicts the operation of both a single-warhead ICBM and a "MIRVed" ICBM.

MIRV stands for Multiple Independently targetable Reentry Vehicle.† The term is complex, but the concept is simple. (See Figure 3.1.) The booster for a

---

*As shown in Figure 3.1, the missile booster is the large section below the warhead which contains the rocket motors and their fuel. Most missile boosters have three sections—called stages—but some have two and some have only one.

†"Multiple" simply means there is more than one warhead. "Independently targetable" means that each of the warheads can be sent to a different target. "Reentry Vehicle" is another name for a missile warhead where the "reentry" part means the warhead will reenter the atmosphere at the end of its trajectory.

FIGURE 3.1
Ballistic Missiles

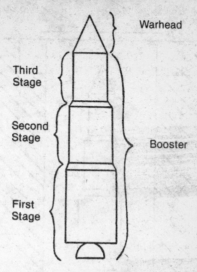

Warhead

Third
Stage

Second
Stage

Booster

First
Stage

Single-Warhead Missile

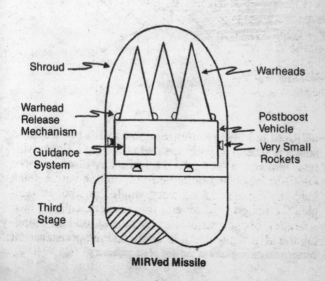

Shroud

Warheads

Warhead
Release
Mechanism

Postboost
Vehicle

Guidance
System

Very Small
Rockets

Third
Stage

MIRVed Missile

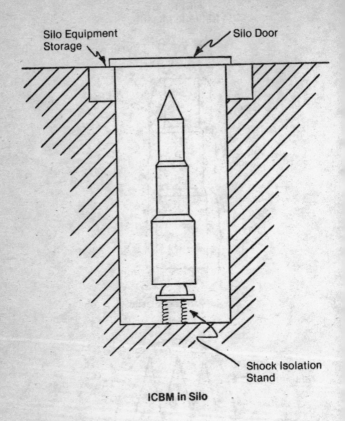

Silo Equipment Storage

Silo Door

Shock Isolation Stand

ICBM in Silo

MIRVed missile operates the same as the booster for a single-warhead missile. Instead of having a single warhead, however, a MIRVed missile has three or more warheads enclosed on a "shroud," along with a small guidance system and a very small "postboost vehicle," equipped with several tiny rockets, called a bus. After the booster stops burning, the shroud surrounding the MIRV payload falls away and the booster itself

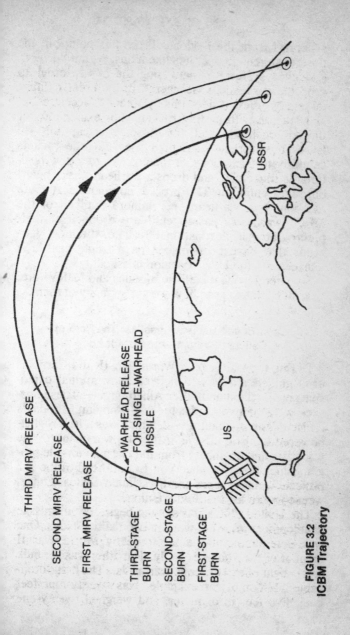

THIRD MIRV RELEASE

SECOND MIRV RELEASE

FIRST MIRV RELEASE

WARHEAD RELEASE
FOR SINGLE-WARHEAD
MISSILE

THIRD-STAGE
BURN

SECOND-STAGE
BURN

FIRST-STAGE
BURN

USSR

US

FIGURE 3.2
ICBM Trajectory

separates from the payload. From this point on, the postboost vehicle operates like a bus, with a "driver" (guidance system) maneuvering the bus in order to drop its warhead "passengers" on different military targets or cities. It does this by steering, accelerating, and braking with its tiny rockets. For example, after the bus positions itself for Moscow, it carefully releases the warhead and then uses its little rockets carefully to back away. It then moves to a new position, or trajectory, and drops a warhead "passenger" on, say, Leningrad. This process continues at the rate of about two warheads per minute until all of the MIRV warhead "passengers" are dropped at their preprogrammed destinations. To date, the most warheads that have been placed on a single missile is fourteen, on the U.S. Poseidon missile.

So much for what ballistic missiles and MIRVs are; now sit back and read how we got so many of them.

Land-Based Ballistic Missiles: The Perfect Delivery System—but Not for Long

During the last year of World War II, the Germans used guided missiles to deliver conventional explosives on England and other Allied targets. These missiles were of two kinds: the V-1—similar to today's cruise missiles—and the V-2, which was a true rocket-powered ballistic missile. After the war many of the scientists and engineers from the German missile program, including Wernher Von Braun, head of the V-2 project, went to work for the United States. Others went to work for the Soviet Union.

The United States was slow to begin serious missile development after the war for two main reasons. One was domination of the air force by World War II bomber pilots who liked to fly. The other was the bulk and weight of early atomic warheads. (The first "droppable" H-bomb, for example, was twenty-four feet long, five feet in diameter, and weighed twenty-one tons.) As American nuclear physicists designed and successfully tested increasingly smaller warheads, however, interest in ballistic missiles grew. Finally, in 1954, the government began an all-out program to develop an intercontinental ballistic missile* (ICBM) for deployment in the United States and an intermediate-range ballistic missile (IRBM) for deployment in Europe.

In August 1957 the Soviet Union announced it had successfully launched a long-range ballistic missile. The reaction of the American defense establishment was relatively mild—the Soviets were always exaggerating their capabilities. Then, in October of 1957, the Soviets launched the first *Sputnik*—and this time the reaction was dramatic, approaching panic. The Pentagon knew from its own work on ballistic missiles that the problems in launching a satellite—meeting the rocket power and guidance system requirements—were technically similar to those of intercontinental ballistic missiles. If the Russians could do one, they almost certainly could do the other.

Sputnik gave renewed momentum to the U.S. ballistic missile program. By the late 1950s the first U.S. ICBMs, called Atlas, were deployed in the continental U.S. and the first IRBMs, called Thor and Jupiter, were deployed in Turkey, Italy, and Great Britain. All of these missiles were large and liquid-fueled, which made them difficult to handle, and all were deployed

---

*There is a complete family of ballistic missiles with names and associated acronyms which reflect their ranges:

Intercontinental Ballistic Missile (ICBM):
  Over 3,000 miles (5,500 km)
Intermediate-Range Ballistic Missile (IRBM):
  1,200–3,000 miles (2,000–5,000 km)
Medium-Range Ballistic Missile (MRBM):
  600–1,200 miles (1,000–2,000 km)
Short-Range Ballistic Missile (SRBM):
  Under 600 miles (1,000 km)

on aboveground launch pads, which made them vulnerable to attack.

The first American ICBM, the Atlas, was quickly superseded by two new missiles: the Titan, another large liquid-fueled missile with a nine-megaton warhead, and the Minuteman, a smaller solid-fueled missile with a one-megaton warhead. Eventually, the Minuteman became the dominant land-based U.S. ICBM because the solid fuel made it safer, easier to move about, and easier to maintain, and because a one-megaton warhead was large enough to destroy most targets in the Soviet Union. In addition, having larger numbers of smaller missiles presents a larger number of targets to the Soviet Union and thereby makes the overall U.S. ground-based missile force less vulnerable.

Today the United States has 1,052 ICBMs—1,000 Minuteman and 52 Titan missiles—all deployed in underground silos.* Like the B-52, the Minuteman has gone through a number of model changes. The Minuteman I was followed by the Minuteman II, another single-warhead missile, and the Minuteman III, a MIRVed missile with three warheads. The current Minuteman force consists of 450 Minuteman IIs and 550 Minuteman IIIs. At one time there were 54 Titans. Of the two no longer operational, the most spectacular loss was the 1980 explosion of a Titan booster at an Arkansas site. For a few hours the nine-megaton warhead could not be found. Any volunteers for a search party?

---

*To understand what an underground silo looks like, simply imagine a giant hand driving a steel and concrete farm silo into the ground. Add some underground communications, electronic and environmental control equipment near the surface, a two-foot-thick concrete door, and you have it. In the United States these silos are located in the middle of farms or ranches in Missouri, Wyoming, the Dakotas, Montana, Kansas, Arkansas, and Arizona. Individual silos are about five miles apart and, if you like, you can walk up to the hundred-foot diameter chain-link fence surrounding each and see the silo door. It's nice country.

As with the B-52, there has been a long search for both a replacement missile for the Minuteman and some method of basing it other than in underground silos. The problem is that technology has caught up with silo-based ICBMs and missile accuracy has now reached the point that silos can be destroyed by opposing ICBMs. We have seen this problem coming for nearly fifteen years but to date have been unable to find another means of basing ICBMs on land that meets the requirements of survivability, reasonable cost, and acceptability to the bulk of the U.S. population.

Our efforts to develop a new ICBM and a new basing mode have been embodied in a program called M-X. The M-X missile design was chosen in 1979, and the first flight test of the missile is scheduled for 1983. The missile will be solid-fueled and capable of carrying up to twelve warheads, although the most likely number will be ten. It will be much more accurate than the Minuteman and capable of destroying Soviet ICBM silos in the same manner that Soviet ICBMs currently threaten U.S. ICBM silos. President Carter wanted to base two hundred M-X missiles in a system of 4,600 hardened shelters in Nevada and Utah. It would have been a gigantic "shell game," with the missiles randomly moved between the shelters by a fleet of outsized trucks, some carrying real missiles and some dummies. This concept was abandoned by the Reagan administration in favor of a plan to deploy one hundred M-X missiles in existing Titan and Minuteman silos.

If you're a betting person, you might want to bet against the current plan coming to pass. No one is very enthusiastic about it. By the time the M-X is ready to be deployed—1986 at the earliest—only one U.S. ICBM silo in ten will be able to survive a Soviet attack. A more likely prospect is the gradual deemphasis of silo-based ICBMs in favor of a new missile-basing plan. The Reagan administration is studying various alternative basing concepts, including aircraft and the previously rejected Nevada/Utah shell game.

They have promised to submit a new basing concept to the nation by 1984.

Soviet ICBM development has generally concentrated on bigger missiles with heavier payloads, at least partly to compensate for the fact that they are less accurate. The Soviets have produced three generations of ICBMs, and they are currently deploying a fourth generation—SS-17s, SS-18s, and SS-19s—all of which are MIRVed. American intelligence analysts believe that a fifth generation of ICBMs is under development, but as of the end of 1981, none of these new missiles has been tested.

The Soviet Union currently has about fourteen hundred ICBMs—all based in underground silos. As indicated above, these ICBMs have the necessary combination of warhead yield and accuracy to destroy most U.S. ICBM silos. The Soviets themselves will face this same ICBM vulnerability problem if and when the U.S. deploys the M-X missile.

The end of the road for silo-based ICBMs is clearly in sight. Although they were once the perfect nuclear weapon delivery vehicle—relatively cheap, easy to handle and maintain, and unobtrusive—the technology of MIRVs and missile accuracy has clearly caught up with them. They will still be around for at least another decade or two, but in time they will go the way of battleships, victims of the irreversible march of technology.

Submarine-Launched Ballistic Missiles: What a Great Idea!

Put ballistic missiles in submarines! When the idea first came up in the mid-1950s, it seemed like a pipe dream. The navy had an early interest in ballistic missiles but planned to launch the missiles from surface ships. Once it became clear that small, safe missiles could be built, however, the attractiveness of submarines as a launch platform led quickly to a vigorous ballistic missile submarine program.

Chosen for this mission were the nuclear-powered submarines which Admiral Hyman Rickover had introduced to the U.S. Navy in the mid-1950s. Because these submarines could remain beneath the surface of the ocean for sixty or more days on patrol, they were virtually undetectable and offered the advantage of getting much closer to enemy territory. As a consequence, the missiles—or, more precisely, the booster section of the missiles—could be much smaller. In addition, proximity to enemy territory reduced missile flight time and therefore enemy reaction or warning time.

The first nuclear-powered ballistic missile submarine (SSBN)* program, called Polaris, was a remarkable success. Missile design technology was progressing so fast that the navy could convert five nuclear-powered submarines already under construction as regular torpedo-armed "attack" submarines into ballistic missile submarines simply by cutting the submarines in half and inserting a missile section.

Between 1959 and 1967 the United States launched forty-one Polaris submarines, each equipped with sixteen missile tubes.† Thirty-nine of the forty-one are still in operation, the other two having simply worn out in spite of frequent maintenance and periodic major overhauls. In the case of submarines, after about twenty to twenty-five years maintenance costs start to be prohibitive. (It's just like trying to maintain

---

*Nuclear-powered ballistic missile submarines are referred to as SSBNs by the navy; "SS" is the navy designation for a submarine, "B" means ballistic missile, and "N" means the submarine is nuclear-powered.

†Submarine missiles are carried vertically and are launched by compressed gas. The missile rocket motor ignites when the missile reaches the surface, and from there on the missile proceeds toward its target just like an ICBM.

a fifteen-year-old American-made car with a hundred thousand miles on it.) As a result, a number of years ago the navy began to build a replacement for Polaris called Trident. The Trident submarine is much bigger than the Polaris. It carries twenty-four launcher tubes, each about 60 percent larger than those of Polaris. This allows a larger missile booster, which means longer range and bigger payload, as well as more ocean to hide in. The first Trident submarine went on patrol in 1981, and present plans call for the construction of another ten to fifteen.

Under normal peacetime conditions, about half of the U.S. ballistic missile submarine force—a total of about three hundred twenty launcher tubes—is at sea at any one time. In a time of serious international crisis, about 80 to 90 percent of the force would be at sea, which is all but those being overhauled.

The Soviets' ballistic missile submarine program has undergone an evolution similar to our own, although they at first deployed a few missiles on some older submarines. The first Soviet submarines specifically designed as missile platforms are referred to as the Yankee class (our term, not theirs). Like Polaris, these submarines carry sixteen launch tubes. (It is often said the Soviets chose this number because they knew the United States had spent millions of dollars to find out what number was best.) Later Soviet missile subs, called the Delta class, carry twelve, sixteen, or eighteen missiles. A giant new submarine now being developed, the Typhoon, will be about as big as the Trident and will probably carry twenty to twenty-four missiles.

Now for the submarine-launched ballistic missiles.

The first Polaris submarine-launched ballistic missiles* (SLBMs) had a range of about 1,500 miles,

---

*In contrast to land-based ballistic missiles, there is no range breakdown for submarine-launched ballistic missiles. They are all referred to as SLBMs, independent of range.

which meant that they had to be launched from the
Norwegian Sea, the Mediterranean, or the Western
Pacific to reach Soviet targets. To maximize their time
at sea, the United States based most of these submarines in Great Britain, Spain, and Guam. Like the
Minuteman, the Polaris missile underwent various
model changes (designated A1, A2, and A3), with
accompanying improvements in range and accuracy.
The final model (still carried on eight submarines) has
a range of 2,500 miles.

In 1970, the United States began replacing Polaris
SLBMs with MIRVed Poseidon SLBMs which can
carry up to fourteen warheads, each with a forty-
kiloton bomb. In practice, however, Poseidon missiles
normally carry ten or fewer warheads. Twenty-five
Polaris submarines are now equipped with Poseidon
missiles. These submarines are often called Polaris/
Poseidon submarines.

The latest U.S. SLBM is called the Trident I. It was
designed to fit inside the cylindrical launch tubes on
Polaris/Poseidon submarines and is currently deployed
on nine of them, as well as on the first Trident submarine. This new missile carries eight warheads, each
with a yield of about one hundred kilotons. Its 4,000-
mile range is approximately twice that of Poseidon,
which means it will be able to strike Soviet targets
from just about any ocean area in the Northern Hemisphere. Eventually twelve of the submarines which
now carry Poseidon will be equipped with the Trident
I.

The navy is currently examining the possibility of
building a new, larger SLBM for deployment in the
large launch tubes on the Trident submarine. This
SLBM, called the Trident II, would carry eight to
twelve warheads and have a range of 6,000 miles.

Soviet SLBM development has followed a pattern
similar to that in the United States. The Soviet SLBM
comparable to Polaris, the SS-N-6, was deployed on
the Yankee-class submarine. It had a single warhead

and a range of about 1,400 miles. The SS-N-6 was followed by the SS-N-8, a 4,000-mile-range single-warhead missile deployed on the early Delta-class submarines. The newest Soviet SLBM, the SS-N-18, has a range of 4,000 miles and can carry six warheads. The Soviets are also testing a new MIRVed SLBM which appears intended for their Typhoon submarine.

Cruise Missiles: New Popularity for an Old Idea

As implied in the title of this section, cruise missiles have had a checkered history as delivery systems. In the person of the V-1s of World War II, they were the first missiles used in modern warfare. They enjoyed a brief resurgence in the mid-50s but lost out to ballistic missiles. Now they are back again, probably to stay.

Before going further, it should be explained what cruise missiles are. Quite simply, they are small pilotless airplanes—miniaturized versions of commercial airliners or jet fighters—with wings that usually fold up for multiple storage and ease of launch. In place of pilots, they are guided to their targets by preprogrammed minicomputers which follow the earth's terrain, generally at low altitudes.

In contrast to those of ballistic missiles, the engines and guidance systems of cruise missiles are always operating.

As with conventional piloted aircraft or ballistic missiles, there is a trade-off between range and payload for cruise missiles. The heavier the payload, the more fuel is required, and the shorter the range. For example, there are two versions of the U.S. Tomahawk cruise missile which can be launched from submarine torpedo tubes. While the two versions appear identical from the outside, one contains a 300-pound, 200-kiloton, nuclear warhead and can go 2,000 miles, while the other is armed with 1,000 pounds of conventional high explosives and has a range of only 350 miles.

Because of their relatively small size, cruise missiles can be launched from submarines, surface ships, airplanes, or mobile ground launchers. The United States is currently refitting B-52 bombers to carry nuclear-armed cruise missiles with a 2,000-mile range. Similar ground-launched cruise missiles are scheduled for deployment in Western Europe in 1983 as part of the controversial modernization and expansion of long-range nuclear forces for NATO.

The Soviet Union has had cruise missiles deployed on bombers and submarines for many years. However, these cruise missiles are considered technically primitive—short-range (about 350 miles), relatively inaccurate, and very large. Soviet technology for producing minicomputers and small jet engines lags substantially behind that of the United States, and it will probably be five to ten years before the Soviets can produce cruise missiles comparable to those currently in production in the United States. In the interim they will continue to be limited to one or two cruise missiles per bomber and large submarine launch tubes like those used for ballistic missiles.

More Numbers

If you want to know more about the bomber and missile systems currently in the American and Soviet inventory, see Appendix C. Information on British, French, and Chinese systems is also provided in that appendix.

The Twin Revolution

In this and the preceding chapters, we have described a twin revolution in (1) the explosive power of nuclear weapons, and (2) the speed, accuracy, and range of nuclear weapon delivery systems. Men have always had the power to kill each other, to destroy cities, and to lay waste cropland. The difference now is that the twin revolution allows us to destroy whole countries in a matter of hours. It is doubtful that the famous German strategist Clausewitz had this in mind when he defined war as the pursuit of politics by other means.

The atomic bomb dropped on Hiroshima had an explosive power of 15 kilotons of TNT, five thousand times more powerful than a conventional bomb of comparable weight. The first hydrogen bomb was detonated only five years later and had an explosive power of one megaton (1,000 kilotons), sixty times more powerful than the Hiroshima bomb. The power of subsequent thermonuclear explosions has been as high as fifty megatons of TNT. Witnesses of atomic explosions even at the kiloton level universally report a mingled sense of awe and horror. The multimegaton weapons simply surpass the capacity of human imagination and comprehension.

This steady process of development, achieved only with great effort and expense, has been just as successful with regard to delivery systems. The B-29 four-engine propeller-driven bomber has been superseded by missiles which can pass between continents in thirty minutes. A single missile can deliver a warhead whose explosive power surpasses that of all of the 2.2 million tons of bombs dropped on Germany in World War II. It can reliably place that warhead within a couple of hundred yards of any target.

As of the end of 1981, the total destructive power of the nuclear weapons of all nations represented ten *tons* of TNT for every man, woman, and child on the face of the earth. Think about that.

4

See How They Run: The Soviet-American Arms Race

Every four years the high drama of athletic competition is merged with international politics on the playing fields of the Olympics. Here we are witness to a grand display of rivalry and scorekeeping in which a country's stature and progress along the path away from barbarism is measured symbolically by the number of gold, silver, and bronze medals which its athletes win. For many of us, the Olympics offer a special one-on-one challenge—the medal competition between the United States and the Soviet Union. And while we are loath to admit it, most of us probably see this quadrennial sporting event as a test of the American way of life—democracy, freedom, and capitalism—against the Soviet alternative of communism, totalitarianism, and state control of production and commerce.

When the United States faces off against the Soviet Union in international competition away from the sporting fields of the Olympics, the nature of the game changes dramatically. There are no universally subscribed to rules, no tightly controlled set of events at carefully selected sites, no neatly dressed officials who place the medals around the necks of the winners as a national anthem sounds triumphantly in the background. Rather, the rules are whatever either side

wishes to make them. The game goes on minute by
minute, year round; the playing field is global; the
stakes are far higher; and in the end, there may be no
winners at all.

The Name of the Game Is the Arms Race

It may come as a surprise, but "the best and the
brightest" minds in this country cannot agree on *why*
there is an arms race. Yes, that's right: there is no
widely accepted explanation of why the United States
and the Soviet Union, who for four years combined
their efforts to defeat a barbarous Nazi state, have
over the last thirty-seven years assembled a nuclear
weapons capability that would enable each to destroy
the other many times over. Many theories or models
have been proposed to describe and explain this competition. They have names like "game theory",
"worst-case analysis," and "action-reaction" and involve terms like "greater-than-expected threat,"
"technological imperative," and "military-industrial
complex" (on both sides). However, no single theory
can explain all, or even the majority, of the strategic
weapons decisions made by the United States and the
Soviet Union since 1945. It's like the economy: if there
does exist a theory that explains past behavior and
helps to predict the future, it certainly is beyond the
ability of current experts to formulate. In fact, many
factors which influence the arms race—the rapid pace
of technology, the uncertainty and impact of economic
and international political conditions, the human element in decision making, and so on—are themselves
so complex and unpredictable that one wonders
whether a comprehensive and comprehensible explanation of the contest is even possible.

Nevertheless, it is clear that some examination of
the causes of the competition is necessary and worth-
while. So, with proper humility, such an effort is
provided below—followed by a summary description

of the competition and some perspectives on what you should glean from this chapter.

What Makes Sammy—and Ivan—Run

In a September 1967 speech delivered in San Francisco, then Secretary of Defense Robert McNamara provided one of the better theories for the Soviet-American arms race. He called it an "action-reaction" phenomenon—first one side builds a weapon, then the other side builds something to counter it. In this way bomber begets bomber, and missile missile. One feature of McNamara's model is that it describes a major element in the military policy of both sides: the effort to point at least as much destructive power at the other fellow as he is pointing at you. If you can't point quite the same things—because you lag in missile technology, say, or the draft is unpopular—then point something else which will serve the same purpose. The result is a kind of perpetual standoff—two heavily armed nations, neither of which can quite get the edge on the other.

Needless to say, there are circles in which McNamara's theoretical model is bitterly criticized. The reason for this hostility is that according to the action-reaction theory, the arms race isn't *about* anything. It just goes, like a perpetual-motion machine. The critics of the action-reaction insist there really isn't an arms *race* at all, in the strict meaning of the word, but something quite different—a threat and a response. Critics in the United States argue that the Soviet Union is expansionist and that the West must arm to defend itself. Soviet critics of the McNamara model think that the West is out to destroy the Soviet Union and communism and that Russia must arm to defend its way of life. Ideology plays no role in the McNamara model, which suggests that the arms race feeds on itself, has no overriding political cause, and can be stopped only once we understand how it works. The us-against-them group takes a darker view: real peace will never come until the tiger changes his stripes and the Russians (or the Americans) abandon their dreams of world revolution (or capitalism triumphant).

Leaving this unresolvable argument for the moment, no one denies that there has been an enormous buildup in arms on both sides and that in making weapons decisions each side pays close attention to the military programs of its rival. This is the job of intelligence, which has been conducted by huge institutions on both sides. The American Central Intelligence Agency (CIA) has at least fifteen thousand full-time employees and a budget of perhaps $1.5 billion a year. The Soviet intelligence services—the KGB and the GRU—are bigger, but probably don't spend as much money. Both sides seem to be good at their work, which helps to keep the situation under control. It is surprise that military men like least, and thanks to accurate intelligence, there have been no *big* surprises in weaponry—by either side—since 1945.

But weapons programs take a long time to develop—at least ten years from an idea scratched out on the back of an envelope to an actual weapon in the field. Because intelligence specialists have a very hard time seeing that far down the road, military planners tend to err on the side of caution, to assume the worst, to prepare for anything. This is referred to as "worst-case analysis," and it seems to be the working rule of thumb on both sides. Since you can't *know* what the other side will have in its arsenal ten years down the road, better play it safe, figure what the other guy *could* do, and plan to be ready for that. After all, this is no idle game—the security of one's nation is at stake.

In trying to estimate Russian military capabilities, the Pentagon has a special category for the worst case called the greater-than-expected threat, or GTET. This threat is extrapolated from an assessment of future Soviet capabilities and intentions—the "expected threat," which is nothing more nor less than what we *really* think they will have. For example, if the U.S.

intelligence gatherers' best estimate is that the Soviet Union will have seven thousand ICBM warheads by 1987, the Pentagon will try to plan U.S. force levels sufficient to meet a somewhat greater number, say eight thousand to ten thousand warheads—just in case.

This systematic overcompensation—called alarmist by some, prudent by others—also reflects each side's fear of possible technological breakthroughs by the other. American defense planners and their Soviet counterparts spend many sleepless nights worrying about how to prepare for some exotic new weapon (a space-based antiballistic missile system using charged particle beams or lasers is one current nightmare—see Chapter 15) that might render existing arms obsolete overnight. Fears of this kind make both sides technologically aggressive. To keep tabs on what the other fellow *might* do requires research in all the possibilities. When the researchers find something that works, pressure naturally builds to go ahead and make it.

Thus the arms race proceeds—steadily, energetically, expensively, and successfully. No other period in human history has been so inventive militarily. Whole generations of weapons have come and gone. This would be a dazzling human achievement, if it weren't for the danger involved. In less than forty years two nations thousands of miles apart have found the means to destroy each other many times over—along with just about everybody else in between. The exhausted warriors of 1945 have turned into giants armed with mighty hammers. This is how it was done.

1946–1950: Jogging Alone

After the defeat of Nazi Germany and Japan, both the United States and the Soviet Union drastically cut back their standing armies. Tensions in the wartime alliance soon blossomed into full-fledged hostility, however, and the arms race began. From the beginning both sides concentrated on what they were good at: the Soviets mobilized vast armies heavy in artillery and tanks, while the U.S. developed technologically sophisticated weaponry, which meant atomic bombs and the means to deliver them.

Atomic bomb production in the United States did not stop with the Japanese surrender, and our late August 1945 inventory of one lone bomb was soon joined by others. By the end of the year we were producing enough fissionable material to make two or three bombs a month. By 1950 the U.S. stockpile was on the order of "several hundred" weapons. (For some inexplicable reason, the exact number is still classified.)

Throughout this period the main U.S. delivery system consisted of modified B-29 bombers, stationed at bases in Greenland, Iceland, Okinawa, Alaska, and Japan, all within striking distance of major Soviet cities. As the cold war progressed, the United States arranged to build other bases on the outer perimeter of the Soviet Union—in Spain, Tunisia, Saudi Arabia, French Morocco, and Turkey. Russia, meanwhile, secured its borders from land invasion by creation of a buffer of satellite states, including—at least until about 1960—a friendly communist government in China. Despite their strength on the ground, the Russians were still threatened by the B-29s in the ring of bases on all sides of the Soviet homeland. In cowboys and Indians terms, we had 'em surrounded—*and* we had The Bomb.

Then, in August of 1949, the Soviet Union exploded its first atomic bomb. While the device was probably too big to be dropped by any Soviet airplane then in existence, it signaled the beginning of the end for the U.S. monopoly on nuclear weapons.

1950–1955: Another Jogger on the Track

The 1950s had a sobering beginning. The fledgling NATO (North Atlantic Treaty Organization) alliance, formed between the U.S. and most Western European nations to combat the expanding strength of the Soviet land army, now had to face the frightening prospect of Russian nuclear weapons. All the experts had thought that the Soviet bomb was two years to a decade away. The U.S. response to its sudden appearance provides the first clear example of the action-reaction phenomenon in the nuclear age. In 1950 President Truman's National Security Council adopted its first comprehensive statement of American military doctrine and strategy. Known as National Security Council Paper No. 68, or NSC 68, it called for "an immediate and large scale buildup in our military and general strength and that of our allies with the intention of righting the balance of power. . . ." The immediate result of the Russian bomb was Truman's decision to build the hydrogen bomb and to speed production of the B-36 bomber. We built a bomb, then the Russians built a bomb, then we built a bigger bomb—and so it went.

In 1950 it was assumed that the Russians were pushing their military programs forward at breakneck speed. U.S. experts were predicting that the Russians would be ahead by 1954. When 1954 actually arrived, it turned out the Soviets had built an estimated three hundred to four hundred nuclear bombs but still lacked a long-range bomber. Our allies in Western Europe were increasingly vulnerable to Soviet medium-range bombers, but the American republic remained safe, protected by the vast oceans which had spared it the extraordinary destruction of two world wars.

1955–1960: Jockeying for Position

At the 1954 Mayday celebration in Moscow, the Soviets unveiled the Bison, their first intercontinental bomber. If you have ever wondered why you were hiding under your school desk during air-raid drills in the mid-1950s, the Bison and its close companion, the Bear, unveiled in 1955, are the reasons. For the first time since the British sacked Washington, D.C., in the War of 1812, the U.S. had become vulnerable to foreign attack. The effect was immediate and profound. The U.S. intelligence community predicted an imminent "bomber gap" in anticipation of a big Soviet push in aircraft production. A special presidential commission secretly reported in 1955 that the U.S. would be wide open to Russian bombers unless something was done. It was. The ICBM program was given the government's highest priority, and production of the B-52, our new intercontinental bomber, was accelerated. The "worst case" was the gospel of the day. By 1958 there was a bomber gap, all right—but it was five to one favoring the United States!

In August of 1957 the Soviet Union successfully tested the first ICBM. Two months later, in October 1957, the same booster was used to launch into orbit *Sputnik*, the first man-made satellite. The immediate effect of this Soviet success was to shift U.S. concern from Soviet bombs to Soviet missiles. The "bomber gap" was replaced by the "missile gap." (This pattern is characteristic of "worst-case" analysis: gaps never seem to go away; they just change their focus.) The reaction of the United States military establishment was dramatic. Within two years U.S. intermediate-range ballistic missiles were placed in Turkey, Germany, Italy, and Great Britain, from which they could reach the Soviet Union. The U.S. ICBM program also received a big boost, and by 1960 more than a hundred Atlas ICBMs had been deployed at sites in the United States.

The public reaction to *Sputnik* was just as dramatic. Broadcasting its beeps from near space, the Soviet satellite proved that Russia was not a backward peasant nation. American complacency received a rude shock. The response of Congress was to increase tremendously funding for education and research in engineering, mathematics, and science. In fact, most members of today's technological community in the

United States can be properly termed children of *Sputnik*.

1960–1965: Sprinting along the Missile Track

Perhaps the most profound effect of *Sputnik* was the broad realization that a "Buck Rogers war"—a push-button war of missiles rather than men—was now on the horizon. The vulnerability of the United States to missile attack became a central issue in the 1960 U.S. presidential campaign after Democratic nominee John Kennedy claimed that a "missile gap" had been allowed to emerge while the White House was in complacent, budget-conscious Republican hands. At the same time, the intelligence analysts were predicting that hundreds of missiles would soon be targeted on the United States. After his election, Kennedy successfully pushed for dramatic increases in spending on our own strategic missile programs—ICBMs and the Polaris submarine-launched ballistic missiles.

Even before the end of 1961, Secretary of Defense McNamara conceded that the "missile gap" had not in fact developed as feared or predicted. Rather than the three hundred to a thousand Soviet ICBMs foreseen at the height of the missile panic, actual counts showed only fifty to a hundred. While "missile gap" fears lasted, however, they were virulent. It was during this period that the U.S. first tried seriously to center its civil defense program on a massive network of urban fallout shelters. The program never won broad national support (see Chapter 5), the frightened public preferring to focus its attention on the dangers of open-air testing of nuclear weapons. Consequently— and only a year after the Cuban missile crisis—the United States, the Soviet Union, and great Britain signed the 1963 Limited Test Ban Treaty prohibiting all weapons tests in the atmosphere, underwater, and in space. Only underground tests were to be permitted, and it is there that over six hundred have taken place.

1965–1970: Flat Out in the Nuclear Olympics

By 1965, it was clear that the United States and the Soviet Union were embarked on a competition in numbers of nuclear weapons and delivery systems for which there was no end in sight. This competition had also expanded to antiballistic missile (ABM) systems as each side sought unsuccessfully to solve the problem which Khrushchev described as "hitting a fly in the sky." Despite the technical difficulties, the "greater-than-expected threat" in ABMs continued to preoccupy U.S. planners fearful of a Soviet breakthrough which would enable them to convert thousands of antibomber air defense interceptors into ABM interceptors.

The all-out missile competition and the race to perfect ABMs provided the setting for the Strategic Arms Limitation Talks (SALT) and the beginning of détente—the effort to establish a more constructive relationship with the Soviet Union. President Johnson first proposed arms talks at a meeting with Premier Kosygin in 1967, and the two nations formally opened the negotiations in Helsinki, Finland, in the fall of 1969, Richard Nixon's first year in office.

The 1960s had begun with the United States holding a formidable 5,000-to-400 advantage over the Soviet Union in nuclear warheads deliverable to the territory of the other side. The U.S. also led in missiles—125 SLBMs and ICBMs to Russia's fifty. At the end of the decade the United States still enjoyed a substantial lead in intercontinental bombers (600 to 150), SLBM launch tubes (656 to 205), and total warheads (6,000 to 1,000). The Russians, however, had pulled ahead in ICBMs (1,350 to 1,054) and in total megatonnage (the combined explosive force in their nuclear arsenal). In addition, the Soviet ICBMs carried a larger payload (or "throw-weight"), raising fears among U.S. analysts that the Soviets would MIRV their big missiles with large numbers of warheads.

While the arsenals of the two superpowers were

growing rapidly, negotiations proceeded slowly. The major achievement of this period was the 1968 signing of the Non-Proliferation Treaty, the first step toward controlling the spread of nuclear weapons beyond the five countries which had already developed them—the United States (1945), the Soviet Union (1949), Great Britain (1952), France (1960), and China (1965).

1970–1975: Time Out

The SALT I negotiations concluded in May 1972 with Leonid Brezhnev and Richard Nixon signing the SALT I agreements—the first major treaty limiting arms since the 1920s. A potential race in ABM systems was stopped in its tracks by a restrictive ABM Treaty, while the so-called Interim Agreement temporarily froze ICBM and SLBM levels on both sides. The world breathed a sigh of relief as the two superpowers ushered in an era of détente. The Doomsday Clock of *The Bulletin of the Atomic Scientists,* founded by alumni of the Manhattan Project in the late 1940s, was moved back to twelve minutes before midnight.*

1975–1980: The End of Détente; the Race Resumes

As the 1970s progressed it became increasingly clear that the Soviets were not only producing large *numbers* of MIRVed ICBMs but were also building a force with sufficient accuracy and destructive power to threaten even targets "hardened" to nuclear weapons effects, such as U.S. silo-based ICBMs. Defense analysts refer to this as a "counterforce capability"—the

---

*This clock has long stood as a symbol of international tensions and the danger of nuclear war. The magazine's board of directors periodically move the clock's hands when world events change the international political climate. It now stands at four minutes to midnight, the closest it has been to the final hour since the Cuban missile crisis.

ability to counter or, more precisely, destroy the military forces of the other side.

The U.S. government, meanwhile, had halted its MIRVed ICBM program and was resisting military pressure to build a large new ICBM to match the big Soviet missiles, largely because it viewed such weapons as destabilizing. Even though SALT I established no limits on MIRVed missiles, it was hoped by many American defense planners that the Russians would also voluntarily exercise restraint in this aspect of their ICBM program, or that the SALT II negotiations would somehow solve the problem. Neither occurred. When SALT II was signed in 1979, it put limits on many categories of arms competition but did nothing to mitigate the threat to American silo-based ICBMs.

In a space of twenty years, silo-based ICBMs had been transformed from the premier weapon of the nuclear age into an obsolescent and increasingly vulnerable monument to the march of technology.

Continued Russian missile building and adventurism, the failure of SALT II to achieve deep reductions in nuclear arms, the political weakness of the Carter presidency, and, finally, the invasion of Afghanistan all combined to prevent Senate ratification of the new arms treaty. Détente was mortally wounded, and the Doomsday Clock moved to four minutes before midnight.

In thirty-seven years of nuclear arms competition, the weapons builders had achieved one triumph after another. The negotiators have signed only a few peripheral agreements, and even those are now threatened. Thus it might be fairly said that the decade of the 1980s began, once again, on square one.

Who's Winning the Arms Race?

The simplest approach to judging a competition in arms—short of war, of course—is what the Pentagon sometimes calls bean counting. So many bombers, so many bombs, and so on. Figure 4.1 provides a twenty-year history of the growth of U.S. and Soviet forces in what are generally agreed to be the three most important categories in the arms race—the number of strategic delivery systems, the number of strategic nuclear warheads, and their explosive power. (Projections to 1990 are also shown.) All numbers refer to the so-called strategic systems*—long-range bombers (sometimes called heavy bombers), ICBM launchers (i.e., silos), and SLBM launchers (i.e., missile tubes on submarines). Appendix C gives a further breakdown in these three categories.

In the first decade of the cold war the bean-counting approach worked, more or less, but the advent of nuclear-armed ICBMs and SLBMs complicated the arithmetic. Variations in reliability, vulnerability to attack, accuracy, and destructive power made comparison even more difficult. Today what is important is not only quantity but also quality. For instance, does a one-megaton Minuteman warhead equal three MIRVed warheads adding up to 600 kilotons? Do long-range SLBMs count more than shorter-range weapons because the subs which carry them have more ocean to hide in? Do ICBMs count more than SLBMs because they're more accurate? Or do SLBMs count more than ICBMs because they get there quicker? One reason arms negotiations are so difficult is that nothing quite "equals" anything else.

Suppose Side A has one hundred 100-kiloton weapons and Side B has fifty 400-kiloton weapons, giving Side A a two-to-one advantage in number of

---

*The term *strategic* is generally used to distinguish long-range nuclear forces from medium-range nuclear forces, which are referred to as *theater* nuclear forces, and short-range nuclear forces, which are referred to as battlefield nuclear forces. Sometimes theater and *battlefield* nuclear forces are grouped with conventional forces in a category called *tactical* nuclear forces.

FIGURE 4.1
The Soviet-American Strategic Arms Race

NOTE: All numbers shown are for ICBMs, SLBMs, and strategic bombers. Equivalent megatons is the most commonly used measure of aggregate explosive power. It is obtained by somewhat upgrading warheads with yields below one megaton and somewhat downgrading those with yields above one megaton.

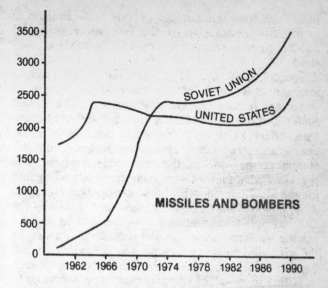

weapons but Side B a two-to-one advantage in explosive yield. Who's "ahead"? Suppose further that A has fifty very large prime targets that might be destroyed by 400-kiloton warheads, while Side B has a hundred small prime targets vulnerable to 100-kiloton weapons. How should A respond if B proposes an arms agreement which, for reasons of "fairness," would limit both sides to equal forces—fifty big weapons each? See the problem?

Advice for Arms-Race Handicappers

Anyone seriously concerned about the threat of nuclear war should take three lessons from this brief history of the arms race.

First, there really *is* an arms race—and right now there is no end in sight. Theories of why it exists are interesting, but our inability to control this obviously dangerous competition gives poignant testimony to their inadequacy. The facts speak for themselves. Since 1945 the United States and the Soviet Union have gone from one nuclear weapon between them to nearly fifty thousand. At the rate we're going, in another forty years the total could be a hundred thousand.

Second, any significant calculation of relative strength must take into consideration a variety of important factors beyond raw numbers. The United States and the Soviet Union are quite different countries, offering different targets and armed with different weapons systems. If anyone makes a blanket statement that one or the other side is ahead, ask precisely what factors were considered in making that judgment. Then ask why other factors were ignored. And, if you want to be very disarming, ask why the U.S. advantages in finding submarines (called antisubmarine warfare capability) and submarine quieting or the profound Soviet advantages in defending against bomber attacks and destroying hardened targets such as ICBM silos—all of which are far more important to deterring war than numbers—have been ignored.

Third, at the moment the strategic strength of both sides is roughly equal, and it is likely to remain so for some time. Even a major effort by one side or the other could not easily upset this balance. Both sides are embarking on large new weapons programs which tend to capture media attention and tend to distract from the real issue—the existence of an arms race that we know is steadily increasing the risk of nuclear war but don't know how to stop.

5

Naked to Mine Enemies: Defense against Nuclear Attack

Once human beings started throwing stones and spears at one another, it wasn't long before someone decided that shields and armor would provide a useful defense against attack. As history progressed better offensive weapons led to better defensive weapons—stockades, castles, armored ships and tanks, antiaircraft guns, and so forth. But offensive weapons have always seemed to be one step ahead of defenses. It is no exception with nuclear weapons.

A Fly in the Sky: Defense against Missile Attack

In a recent public opinion survey on defense issues, over half of the respondents expressed a belief that the United States had a defense system against ballistic missile attacks—a so-called antiballistic missile or ABM system.* They were wrong. We do not have an ABM system, and there is no prospect of one emerging in the foreseeable future.

---

*ABM systems generally consist of interceptor missiles and two types of radars. The first radar has a large flat face about the size of a football field (tilted on its side). Its job is to detect an incoming missile warhead as it appears over the horizon (hundreds of miles

The Russians are in about the same situation as the
United States. A few dozen ABM interceptor missiles
have been deployed around Moscow since 1964, but
the system was not very effective then, and is certainly not effective against today's modern missiles.

The ABM difficulty was once characterized by Soviet leader Nikita Khrushchev as trying "to hit a fly in
the sky." He was right. The problem is similar to
trying to hit a baseball in flight with another baseball.
If you were Willie Mays and you practiced a lot, you
might be able to do it, at best, maybe half the time. It is
doubtful that the best ABM system could improve
much on that percentage—which is not good enough if
you're trying to defend a city. ABM is simply an
extraordinarily difficult problem, and, in spite of the
expenditure of billions of dollars over the last twenty
years, no reliable means of shooting down incoming
missiles is in sight.

Our shared inability to perfect an effective ABM
system is one of the reasons the United States and the
Soviet Union agreed to the SALT I "ABM Treaty,"
which limits both sides to very, very small ABM
deployments. Each side is currently permitted only
one ABM battery with a hundred ABM interceptor
missiles—hardly a challenge to the thousands of warheads in today's arsenals.

Both the United States and the Soviet Union are
continuing to spend hundreds of millions of dollars

---

away) and plot its course. The second radar then guides an interceptor missile to a calculated point in space where it blows up the
incoming warhead. The factors that make this problem difficult
include (1) the difficulty of detecting the incoming warhead; (2) the
speed of the incoming warhead—10,000 miles per hour; (3) the
likelihood that many warheads will be attacking at the same time;
(4) the blinding of the radars—called blackout—when a nuclear
weapon explodes in the upper atmosphere; (5) the imperfect reliability of ABM interceptor missiles—at best, about 80 percent; and
(6) the cost of radars and interceptors compared to attacking
warheads.

each year on ABM development programs. We have essentially given up on the problem of defending cities against missile attacks but are examining the possibility of deploying an ABM system that could defend hardened targets such as ICBM silos. In principle, this is an easier task than defending cities—but you still have to hit the fly in the sky.

There is some hope that in the distant future, a space-based ABM system might be developed. Such a system would use lasers or so-called particle beam weapons on Earth-orbiting satellites to shoot down missiles during the first few minutes after launch— before the booster has released its warhead(s). This prospect is discussed in Chapter 15.

Where'd He Go?: Defense against Bomber Attack

The problem of defending against bomber attack is less challenging than the ABM problem but still very difficult, especially because the bomber can change course, fly slower or faster, fly higher or lower, and so forth.*

In the 1950s, when long-range bombers posed the major nuclear threat, both the United States and the Soviet Union built very large air defense systems. Ours had names like Nike and Hercules and were deployed around cities and across our northern borders. As the ballistic missile threat emerged and we

---

*Bomber defenses (called air defense systems) generally consist of a system of radars and interceptor missiles plus fighter aircraft. Sometimes the radars for detecting bombers are placed on airplanes, as in the U.S. AWACS (Airborne Warning and Control System). Similarly, the radars that guide fighter planes to the vicinity of the attacking bomber are usually mounted on the planes themselves. These same components would be used to shoot down cruise missiles.

saw no way to defend against it, we essentially abandoned our air defense systems. Today, there are a few squadrons of fighter aircraft in the U.S. that can do little more than protect us against an attack by, say, Cuba.

On the other hand, the Soviet Union has maintained a very large air defense system. We sometimes wonder why, since it is clearly incapable of stopping a missile attack. In addition, U.S. bombers can penetrate these Soviet air defenses by flying low, "jamming" the Soviet air defense radars with electronic signals, launching cruise missiles from outside the reach of interceptor missiles or fighters, and so forth. Nevertheless, as Soviet air defenses improve, U.S. bombers and their armaments must also improve to ensure that they can penetrate to their targets.

Would You Shoot Your Neighbor?: The Challenge of Civil Defense

In the late 1950s and early 1960s, when Soviet development of intercontinental bombers and intercontinental missiles made the United States vulnerable to nuclear attack, the idea of civil defense became quite popular. (Early civil defense efforts focused on protecting population from nuclear weapons effects, but it should be noted that this term is also applied to protection of industry.) Particular emphasis was given to building fallout shelters in the basements of homes and commercial buildings, subways, and so forth.

The debates in the U.S. in the early 1960s raised questions such as: "If you were in your fallout shelter with your family and no extra provisions, would you shoot your neighbor if he tried to get in?" Popular support for civil defense did not last long. The growth in Soviet missile forces and the staggering expense of building effective shelters made it obvious that civil defense measures to protect people in cities were fruitless.

A U.S. civil defense program (about $200 million per year in federal funds) still exists, but in recent years its main efforts have focused on responding to natural disasters such as floods and earthquakes.

The Soviet Union has a much larger civil defense program, but there is substantial debate about its effectiveness. The Soviet program has two major components: (1) a plan for evacuation of major Soviet cities, and (2) a program for building underground concrete-reinforced shelters for factory workers.

The plan for evacuating Moscow calls for most of the population to walk out of the city, since there is inadequate transportation to move eight million people by train, bus, or auto. This would take three to seven days, and we would discover almost immediately that it was happening. Since this would imply that Soviet authorities thought that nuclear was was imminent, it is likely that spontaneous evacuation of U.S. cities would also take place. (It would be much easier for us to do this because of the large number of U.S. automobiles.) Soviet city dwellers would go to designated rural areas for regrouping, and some method of feeding and sheltering all these people would have to be found. This task would be a difficult one under any conditions, but especially so in winter. Not surprisingly, many experts doubt that this system would work very well amid the breakdown of social order, disruption of services, and so forth that would accompany a nuclear war.

The Soviet program for protecting workers in hardened shelters is also viewed with skepticism. The shelters are usually on the sites of major factories, almost all of which are targeted by U.S. warheads. Workers in such shelters would have a difficult time surviving the multitude of nuclear weapons effects they would be subjected to: blast, burial of their shelters under tons of rubble, fire storms and conflagrations that literally suck the air out of their shelters, denying them oxygen and raising temperatures to intolerable levels.

From the American viewpoint, the biggest problem posed by the Soviet program is the possibility that Soviet decision makers might trust their civil defense system to work—i.e., assume that instead of losing 40 percent of their population, they might lose only, say, 10 percent—and, therefore, be less reluctant to attack the United States or otherwise risk a nuclear war. Soviet cities and military capability would, of course, still be destroyed.

Would you take greater risks or make nuclear-war-related decisions differently if you thought you could move most of your urban population out to the countryside? How about if it were winter?

PART II

The Bomb That's Coming to Dinner

6

It's Them or Us:
A Short History of a
One-Sided Nuclear War

"All Indians walk in single file; at least, the one I saw did!" That object lesson in the problem of generalizations based on a single experience is important to keep in mind as one reads about the only nuclear war the world has ever seen. It was short (three days long), very one-sided (only one side had and used nuclear weapons), and—by today's "standards"—very modest (only two nuclear weapons were exploded). Nevertheless, the experience provides precious insight into *a* nuclear war and how it occurred—the prevailing military situation, the human element, the domestic political factors, the impact of international prestige, and the seeming technological imperative. Try to put yourself in Harry Truman's position—and try to forget that in the only nuclear war we've ever had, *every* one of the nuclear weapons available was used. "All Indians . . ."

A Well-Kept Secret

On April 12, 1945, just three days after the death of Franklin D. Roosevelt, the new president, Harry S. Truman, was given a top-secret briefing by Secretary of War Henry Stimson. The subject was the Manhattan Project, and Truman was hearing about it for the first time. At a secret laboratory in New Mexico,

Stimson told the president, work was rapidly nearing completion on a weapon of vast new destructive power—the atomic bomb. The war in Europe had already ended, but Japan seemed determined to fight until the end. If the bomb were as powerful as the scientists predicted, it might shorten the war by a year. Only Truman could decide whether to use it, where, and how.

In order to guarantee secrecy, only a handful of Roosevelt's staff had been told about the development of atomic weapons at Los Alamos and other secret sites since 1942. By the time Truman became president, the project had built up tremendous momentum and was near success. Money was being spent at the rate of a billion dollars a year, and ten thousand employees were at work developing the bomb mechanism and the fission fuel for the explosion. The Manhattan Project's chief scientist, J. Robert Oppenheimer, claimed that a workable bomb would be ready in a few months' time.

At the end of his briefing on April 12, Stimson recommended that a committee of top scientific, military, and governmental officials be established—in Truman's words—to "study with great care the implications the new weapon might have for us." Truman agreed and appointed a group of top-level military and civilian personnel, called the Interim Committee, which in turn established an advisory committee composed of the principal scientists connected with the Manhattan Project, including Robert Oppenheimer, head of the Los Alamos laboratory.

The Military Situation

After its defeats at Midway, Port Moresby, and Guadalcanal, Japan had gone on the strategic defensive in an attempt to hold the vast territories it had already conquered. The United States and its allies, determined to push Japan from the occupied area, had launched major campaigns on a number of fronts across the Pacific. These counterattacks were successful, and by mid-1944 Japan had lost substantial territory, and disenchantment with the war was rapidly growing in the Japanese homeland. The war economy had begun to flag, fleet and air forces had been critically weakened, and both the political-military establishment and the people of Japan were losing confidence in an eventual victory. As a result a new Japanese government was formed—one which included a number of ministers who favored negotiated surrender.

In late 1944 and early 1945, as the war in Europe was drawing to a close, U.S. military efforts were shifting toward Japan. In Europe the U.S. 8th Air Force, based in Britain, had followed a policy of daylight raids on selected targets—ball-bearing factories, dry docks, railroad marshaling yards, petroleum refineries, and other strategic targets considered critical for the war effort. But experience showed that these targets were hard to hit, that the attacks were only marginally effective, and that the cost was high in terms of planes shot down—averaging between 2 and 3 percent per raid. Consequently, a new policy called area bombing was adopted to hasten the end of the war in the Pacific. The new policy called for a deliberate attempt to create fire storms in Japanese cities—general conflagrations so intense they created 200-mile-per-hour winds on the ground as the air rushed in to feed the fire. In the spring of 1945 two mass raids by B-29 bombers carrying incendiary bombs destroyed sixteen square miles of Tokyo and killed a quarter of a million people.

As the Interim Committee appointed by Truman went to work, the question before it—and the president himself—was not whether terror or the killing of hundreds of thousands of civilians was an acceptable policy; that had already been decided by the incendiary raids. The real question was what effect use of the bomb would have on the postwar world.

Reenter the Scientists

The long-term impact of the use of nuclear weapons in the war was a subject a number of atomic scientists had already been thinking about for some time. The Danish physicist Niels Bohr was convinced that the only hope for avoiding a postwar nuclear arms race was to involve the Russians in attempts at international control. In May 1944 he arranged to see British Prime Minister Winston Churchill in London, but the meeting did not go well. Churchill had a hard time understanding Bohr and didn't like what he heard. At the end of the meeting he told Bohr, ". . . this new bomb is just going to be bigger than our present bombs. It involves no difference in the principles of war. And as for any postwar problems, there are none that cannot be amicably settled between me and my friend, President Roosevelt."

In the United States the Hungarian-born physicist Leo Szilard, who had persuaded Einstein to send Roosevelt a letter about the bomb back in 1939, also arranged to see Roosevelt to warn of the dangers posed by the new weapon. But Roosevelt died before the meeting could take place, and Truman passed Szilard on to an aide.

In Chicago a group of scientists and technicians who knew of the Manhattan Project held a series of meetings and concluded that the United States should demonstrate the bomb—perhaps in Tokyo Bay— before deciding to drop it on a city. The group's report said the only real secret was whether a bomb *could* be made and predicted that "the race for nuclear armaments will be on in earnest not later than the morning after our first demonstration of the existence of nuclear weapons." The group's report was bottled up by the simple expedient of classifying it.

Sifting the Options

Stimson, too, had been worrying about these matters. In late September of 1944, two of his scientific advisers told him a bomb would be ready by August 1, 1945, that the American monopoly would not last more than three or four years, and that atomic weapons would soon be followed by thermonuclear devices of still greater power.

The Interim Committee fully considered proposals to demonstrate the bomb away from the civilian population, an idea which had popped up in many places at once, but the committee's advisers had concluded that no mere technical demonstration would be likely to bring an end to the war and that direct military use was therefore necessary. For one thing, it was argued, the bomb might not work. If it failed after being announced in advance, the Japanese might be encouraged to continue the war. It was also feared that the Japanese might crowd the target site with prisoners of war. A third consideration—one not often addressed directly but obviously much on the minds of committee members—was its effect on the Russians. After his meeting with Truman's aide in May 1945, Szilard reported the prevailing view as being "that our possessing and demonstrating the bomb would make Russia more manageable in Europe."

At its meeting on May 31, 1945, Oppenheimer told the Interim Committee that new and bigger bombs were coming up—up to a hundred megatons in size. But the committee reached the conclusion that the bomb should be used (1) against the enemy, (2) without warning, (3) against a target that would give clear evidence of its tremendous destructive power, and (4) as soon as possible. On June 1, their recommendations were conveyed to President Truman.

Secretary of War Stimson fully agreed with the committee's recommendations but insisted that Kyoto, Japan's cultural capital, be struck from the target list. Hiroshima, so far untouched by the war, was chosen for the first bomb.

In mid-June of 1945, the secretary of war, the secretary of the navy, and the Joint Chiefs of Staff presented their plan for the defeat of Japan to Truman for his approval. The plan called for a two-phase invasion of the Japanese islands to begin in the fall of 1945. The first phase would involve an amphibious landing on one of the southernmost Japanese islands, Kyushu. Four months later, there would be a second invasion of the main island, Honshu, on which Tokyo was located. Military leaders estimated that the defeat of Japan by invasion and conquest would kill or wound one million Americans—General Douglas MacArthur estimated half a million dead—and take until the late fall of 1946 to achieve.

The Situation in Japan

In late June 1945 a new Japanese government headed by Admiral Suzuki was formed. The Suzuki government began an effort to reach a negotiated peace, using the Russians as mediators. The Japanese proposal contained two conditions: (1) retention of conquered areas by Japan, and (2) assurances that the emperor could retain his throne. The initiative was rejected by the United States and its allies, who insisted on unconditional surrender.

By mid-July the Japanese military had in effect already lost the war. The Japanese navy was almost completely destroyed, and the air force reduced to kamikaze attacks with the few planes still left. Only the Japanese army, which numbered about five million, still had any real fighting potential. The American air force and navy could now virtually bomb or shell the Japanese mainland at will, but so long as the Japanese army and the high command were determined to die defending the homeland the last phase of the war promised to be bloody and expensive.

Potsdam

On July 15, 1945, Truman, Churchill, and Soviet leader Josef Stalin met at Potsdam, Germany, to discuss peace in Europe and war in the Pacific. On July 16, as the conference got under way, Secretary of War Stimson cabled Truman in Potsdam with news of the successful atomic test at Alamogordo.

Truman and Churchill decided the time had come to tell Stalin, but to keep it simple. Truman described the moment in his memoirs: "I casually mentioned to Stalin that we had a new weapon of unusual destructive force. The Russian premier showed no special interest. All he said was that he was glad to hear it and hoped we would 'make good use of it' against the Japanese." Stalin's calm was only a facade. He knew about the Manhattan Project and had already begun a Soviet atomic weapons program.

On July 26, 1945, the three leaders issued the Potsdam Ultimatum, which called upon Japan to surrender unconditionally. The document made no mention of the existence or power of the newly acquired U.S. atomic bomb. Three days later, Japanese Premier Suzuki refused the call for surrender, scorning it as "unworthy of public notice."

Dissenting Voices

While Truman was in Potsdam, opposition to using the bomb was being mobilized among the community of Manhattan Project scientists. Leo Szilard and his colleagues drew up a petition with seventy signatures urging Truman not to use the bomb unless the Japanese were told of its full destructive potential and then still refused to surrender. This and other petitions, along with a poll of 150 scientists who argued in favor of a military demonstration before the bomb was used against a city, were placed in a packet and forwarded to the military commander of the Manhattan Project, General Leslie Groves, on July 25, 1945. Groves favored unconditional use of the new weapon, however, and did not deliver this packet to Secretary of War Stimson until August 1, 1945, just five days prior to the bombing of Hiroshima. By this time, Truman was on his way home from the Potsdam Conference on the U.S.S. *Augusta* and accessible only by cable. It was not until eighteen years later that Szilard learned Truman had never been told of the scientists' advice. But it would have made no difference. Truman had already made up his mind.

Hiroshima and Nagasaki

On the morning of August 6, 1945, an American B-29 named *Enola Gay* appeared over the city of Hiroshima. An air-raid siren had sounded a warning, but it was soon followed by an all-clear signal, for only three planes appeared overhead and the Japanese thought it was a reconnaissance flight.

The bomb was dropped by parachute. Many people watched it float slowly toward earth, wondering what it could be. It exploded at 8:15 A.M.

On August 8 Russia declared war on Japan. In Tokyo it was still not known what had happened in Hiroshima. The following day, three days after the bombing of Hiroshima, a second bomb was dropped on Nagasaki. Two days later—after securing an American promise that the emperor would not be overthrown—the Japanese surrendered. Thus ended the first nuclear war.

A Retrospective

Close examination of critical historical events almost always stimulates a host of "what if . . ." speculations. Some of these questions focus on conditions that might have affected key decisions: What if Roosevelt had lived? What if the scientists had gotten to see Truman? What if the Russians had joined the war against Japan immediately after the defeat of Hitler?

For the purposes of this book, the more interesting questions have to do with what the past thirty-seven years would have been like had Hiroshima and Nagasaki not been used as demonstration projects. Would the U.S.-Soviet nuclear arms competition have been more or less intense? Would we have gotten into other nuclear wars—over Berlin, perhaps, or Cuba? Would you be reading this book?

But Hiroshima and Nagasaki *did* occur, and there is much that can be learned from the experience. Some of it is in insight to political decision making as described in this chapter. But the most important is simply there in the pictures—not of specially constructed houses and plastic dummies blown away by a test in the Nevada desert or some South Pacific Island, but pictures of a real city, real workplaces, real homes, real people. Nuclear war can happen. It *has* happened.

7

On the Brink: The Story of the Cuban Missile Crisis

It was the fall of 1962. The New York Yankees were en route to another American League pennant, John F. Kennedy was in his second year as the thirty-fifth president of the United States, and the long cold war between the United States and the Soviet Union was in one of its coldest phases. In the period since 1945 the former World War II allies had challenged each other repeatedly, but never had they come to the brink of nuclear war. All that changed in the fall of 1962 when the Soviet Union tried to deploy nuclear-armed missiles in Cuba.

Berlin and the Bay of Pigs: Ice for the Cold War

In April of 1961 the CIA had clumsily tried to invade Cuba with a thousand courageous but outgunned rebels who were killed or captured on the beach at the Bay of Pigs. Kennedy felt himself humiliated by this catastrophe of bad planning and irresolution. Later that year, at a summit meeting with Khrushchev in Vienna, Austria, the Russian premier stormed and shouted in an obvious attempt to bully the young president. In August the Russians and East Germans caught the Americans by surprise when they suddenly began to erect a wall of cinder blocks and barbed wire through the heart of Berlin, closing off the Soviet zone. In 1962 Berlin and Cuba were the running sores of international affairs, with both sides probing and testing. The United States mounted a secret campaign of sabotage against Cuba with orders to the CIA to wreck the Cuban economy, foment resistance to the regime of Fidel Castro, and—if possible—assassinate the Cuban leader.

Troubling Signals: They Wouldn't Dare!

Throughout the summer of 1962, Russia engaged in a steady and massive buildup of conventional military equipment on the island of Cuba, the Soviet Union's "Communist showcase" in the Western Hemisphere. The buildup was closely monitored by the CIA, and news of it began to leak to reporters. When New York's Senator Kenneth Keating charged that the Russians were planning to put nuclear missiles into Cuba, the administration flatly denied the existence of evidence to support such charges. Fearful that the arms buildup would hurt the Democrats in the congressional elections in November, however, Kennedy moved through diplomatic channels to warn the Soviet leadership that the United States was extremely concerned with Soviet actions in Cuba.

In a private meeting with Attorney General Robert Kennedy on September 4, Russian Ambassador to Washington Anatoly Dobrynin promised that the Soviet Union would do nothing in Cuba to aggravate the international situation during the election campaign. Shortly thereafter the president acknowledged the Soviet message, issuing a stiff and explicit warning that the introduction of offensive strategic nuclear weapons in Club would raise the "gravest issue," but not acknowledging Soviet resentment of U.S. offensive missiles deployed in Turkey and Western Europe and pointed at the Soviet Union. A few days later, the White House received a response from the Kremlin to the effect that no missile capable of reaching the United States would be placed in Cuba.

Although Theodore Sorensen, special counsel to the President, received assurances from Dobrynin similar to those given to Robert Kennedy, he was not quite convinced Dobrynin was telling the truth. The buildup was of a massive scale, and certain construction sites were suspicious. But Dobrynin stuck to his guns: Soviet aid to Cuba was purely defensive in nature.

Kennedy remained suspicious, however, and decided to press the point yet again. On September 13 he gave a major public address in which he drew an explicit distinction between "offensive" and "defensive" weapons. Kennedy pointed out that there was no reason to believe the Soviets intended to place nuclear weapons of any kind in Cuba, but he warned that if they did so a "serious situation" would arise. The Soviet Union again responded, both officially and unofficially, that it clearly understood the American position and would do nothing to worsen the international situation.

Mounting Evidence: Say It Isn't So

Inside the administration the debate continued. In the second week of September a cloud cover settled over the western end of Cuba, obscuring the area where the troubling construction was taking place and inhibiting U.S. ability to keep track of the buildup with overflights by U-2 reconnaissance planes. Eyewitness reports from Cuban refugees arriving in Florida described huge crates being unloaded from Russian ships, trucks carrying long, mysterious objects, and even missiles themselves. One group of analysts said the refugees, unsophisticated in military matters, had only seen air defense missiles for shooting down aircraft. Another group took a darker view.

In an attempt to settle the matter, CIA Director John

McCone asked the United States Intelligence Board (USIB) to evaluate the evidence. On September 19 the board reported its unanimous conclusion: there was no clear evidence of nuclear missiles in Cuba, the Soviets had nothing to gain from such a provocative act, the buildup simply *had* to be defensive in nature, just as the Russians claimed. But McCone was not convinced. He ordered the USIB to go over the issue. The answer on September 20 was the same: there were no Soviet missiles in Cuba.

In the Crisis: Eyeball to Eyeball

It was the middle of October before the skies over Cuba finally cleared. On October 14, the first U-2 reconnaissance mission in nearly a month was sent over the island. The photographs it brought back were unmistakable: Russian engineers were feverishly building launch pads for missiles, and even some of the missiles themselves were visible enough to be easily identified. The missiles that the Soviets were deploying were the SS-4, whose 1,200-mile range put it within reach of Washington, and the SS-5, whose 2,200-mile range made it capable of striking every major American city except Seattle. Having previously obtained operational manuals for both these missiles from a highly placed Soviet spy, Colonel Oleg Penkovskiy, the CIA could follow the engineer's progress on an almost daily basis. The pattern was also identical to that observed in the construction of SS-4 and SS-5 launch pads in the Soviet Union.

Kennedy was shocked and angered by the blatant Soviet deception. The presence of the missiles represented a direct challenge to his explicit warning that such a situation would have "grave consequences." Khrushchev obviously thought Kennedy was weak and could be pushed around. The president felt he could not ignore the provocation, but he decided to keep the information secret until his advisers could decide what to do.

To deal with the crisis, Kennedy called together a special Executive Committee to hammer out the American response. The ExCom, as it came to be known, was comprised of top military and foreign policy advisers, including Secretary of State Dean Rusk, Secretary of Defense Robert McNamara, Attorney General Robert Kennedy, National Security Adviser McGeorge Bundy, Undersecretary of State George Ball, and the Joint Chiefs of Staff.

For a week ExCom held secret meetings at the White House. By carefully disguising their movements ExCom avoided provoking media interest, keeping news of the missile sites out of the press and confined to a small official circle in Washington. The problem of what to do was agonizing. At first the advisers favored a sudden "surgical" air strike to destroy the missiles and launch pads on the ground. There were two problems with this approach: the air force could not guarantee it would destroy all the missiles in a single strike, and there was no way to avoid killing many Russians. A surprise attack would push Khrushchev to the wall, and no one could predict how he would react. The probability of a retaliatory strike against U.S. forces in Europe could not be discounted. Even a Soviet strike against U.S. cities was possible.

"I will always remember Dean Acheson coming into our meeting," Theodore Sorensen said later, "and saying that he felt we should knock out Soviet missiles in Cuba by an air strike. Someone asked him, 'If we do that, what do you think the Soviet Union will do?' He said, 'I think I know the Soviet Union well. I know what they are required to do in the light of their history and their posture around the world. I think they will knock out our missiles in Turkey.' And then the question came again. 'Well, what do we do?' 'Well,' he said, 'I believe under our NATO treaty with which I was associated, we would be required to respond by knocking out a missile based inside the Soviet Union.' 'Well, then what do they do?' 'Well,' he said, 'then that's when we hope cooler heads will prevail and they'll stop and talk.' "

As the days passed, enthusiasm for the "surgical" strike began to wane. The concept of a more gradual approach, one which would give Khrushchev time to think things over before acting, was adopted. During this period the president deliberately stayed away from ExCom meetings. He wanted to ensure an evaluation of the alternatives uninhibited by his presence. But the decision remained his, and Robert Kennedy would remember later the president's agony as he approached the moment when he would have to make up his mind. Like everyone else, he knew the result might be war.

Finally, on October 23, 1962, President Kennedy appeared on national television to describe the situation and how he intended to deal with it. He made it clear that the United States would not tolerate Russian offensive missiles in Cuba. He announced a "quarantine" of Cuba and said no more Russian ships carrying military matériel would be allowed access to the island until the missiles had been removed. He deliberately avoided use of the provocative word "blockade," since that would have been considered an act of war under international law.

He sternly warned the Soviets that "it shall be the policy of this nation to regard any nuclear missile launched from Cuba against any nation in the Western Hemisphere as an attack by the Soviet Union on the United States requiring a full retaliatory response upon the Soviet Union." These were strong and frightening words—"fightin' words" in the Old West—since they threatened nuclear war. They ran through the minds of all Americans with great intensity over the following days as the president and the country waited for the Soviet response.

At first the Soviet position was unclear. Official statements from Moscow stressed the danger of war, repeated claims that the Cuban arms buildup was strictly defensive in nature, and insisted that the Soviets would not recognize a quarantine. Khrushchev himself sent a number of somber but unconciliatory private communications to Kennedy. Meanwhile Soviet ships were approaching Cuba, with missile crates visible on their decks. Kennedy ordered the navy to pull back closer to Cuba to give Moscow more time. At the same time Washington insisted it would resort to force if the Soviets tried to run the quarantine.

Resolution: The Other Guy Blinks

Like a fever, the crisis finally broke. Robert Kennedy suggested that the U.S. respond to a conciliatory message from Khrushchev and ignore a much more pugnacious cable that arrived the following day. The approach worked. On October 26, the Soviet ships stopped dead in the water and then slowly turned around. As Secretary of State Dean Rusk would later relate, "We were eyeball to eyeball and I think the other guy just blinked."

Negotiations continued, and a deal was finally worked out. The Soviets promised to remove all their missiles, just as Kennedy had insisted. The United States pledged not to repeat its attempt to invade Cuba, allowing Khrushchev to claim that he had achieved his principal goal of safeguarding Castro's socialist regime. Later the United States removed its own intermediate-range ballistic missiles in Turkey, but Washington maintained this was not the result of a secret agreement with Russia and had nothing to do with the October crisis.

The Aftermath: Lessons for Both Sides

The Cuban missile crisis proved to be one of the finest hours of Kennedy's administration. The challenge was met firmly but cautiously. Kennedy proved he was no pushover. But for ordinary people everywhere the awful week of confrontation was deeply frightening. Robert Kennedy would later relate in his book *Thirteen Days, The Story of the Cuban Missile Crisis* just how excruciatingly close we came to nuclear war. Both sides had peered over the precipice of nuclear war, and each had made the decision to step back.

The historical consequences of the crisis were far-reaching. Ten months later, the Limited Test Ban Treaty prohibiting nuclear weapons testing in the atmosphere, in space, and underwater was signed by the United States, Great Britain, and the Soviet Union. A separate agreement was reached to establish a direct communications link between the White House and the Kremlin—the so-called Hot Line. Most important of all, both sides learned that war is possible in the nuclear age. The result was a new caution and sobriety in Soviet-American relations. Khrushchev's recklessness, in fact, was one reason for his ouster two years later.

But there was another important result, as well. At the time of the Cuban missile crisis the Soviets were at a profound disadvantage in terms of nuclear capability. Russia had only a handful of ICBMs, and its intercontinental bombers could carry at most a few hundred nuclear weapons. We could have delivered over six thousand nuclear weapons onto Soviet territory, including several hundred ICBMs. The Russians were truly in a position of nuclear inferiority, and they paid for it in their Cuban failure. As Soviet Deputy Foreign Minister Vasily Kuznetsov left one meeting to arrange the departure of the missiles, he remarked to an American negotiator, "You'll never be able to do this to us again."

Kuznetsov was certainly right on one count. As a result of the ensuing Soviet nuclear arms buildup, never again will there be a crisis in which either side possesses anything like the twenty- or thirty-to-one advantage in deliverable nuclear warheads that the U.S. enjoyed at the time of the Cuban missile crisis.

Who will blink the next time? Maybe nobody.

8

Four Simple, Easy-to-Use Scenarios for Killing 500 Million People

"War-gamers" (that's what they're called) in Washington—and probably in Moscow, too—have fought many nuclear wars in the last three decades. Indeed, a group attached to the Office of the Joint Chiefs of Staff in the Pentagon does very little else. Some of their nuclear war games are elaborate, involving high officials as participants and taking weeks to play. Others are begun and finished in the course of a weekend. Some have only a Red Team (the Soviet Union) and a Blue Team (the United States); others have Chinese, British, French, and German teams. But almost all these games have one characteristic in common: they are hard to start. That's right; no one wants to be the first to use nuclear weapons. Why? It's because in a world in which several parties have nuclear arms the result is always the same: destruction of the aggressor and the victim alike. The war-gamers, like everybody else, have concluded that starting a nuclear war doesn't make sense.

Americans have been involved in two large wars since 1945, in Korea and Vietnam. More than eighty thousand Americans were killed in those wars and many times that number wounded. Neither war ended in a clear-cut American victory. On several occasions the Pentagon "suggested," if it did not quite formally recommend, that the United States use nuclear weapons to solve problems on the battlefield—principally in Korea in November of 1950, when Chinese forces crossed the Yalu River and endangered the American army under General Douglas MacArthur, and in the fall of 1968 in Vietnam, when a large force of marines was under seige at Khe Sanh. But American presidents turned down these and other suggestions for the use of nuclear weapons because they felt the danger of escalation far outweighed any possible gain.

Some analysts have even argued that postwar history suggests nuclear weapons will never be used again. Hiroshima and Nagasaki, they say, were the exception, not the rule. World opinion and the threat of international escalation prevents the use of nuclear weapons against opponents who don't have them, and fear of retaliation prevents their use against opponents who do. The result, these analysts claim, is a kind of nuclear stalemate. The Bomb is too dangerous to use in war. In short, deterrence works.

But will this aversion to the use of nuclear weapons continue? The fact remains that nuclear weapons *have* been used—against Japan—and that the United States and the Soviet Union came within a cat's whisker of nuclear war over Cuba in 1962. If mankind's fear of nuclear weapons is a guarantee against their use, we should all be able to stop worrying, because the prospect of even a limited nuclear war is one of suffering and destruction that challenges the human imagination. In a world marked by bickering that quickly escalates into fistfights, however, is the sheer horror of an ultimate conflict enough to keep it from happening?

War has its own pathology: once begun, it is hard to stop. Little wars almost inevitably become big wars, and big wars tend to go to the limit. The world is an unruly place, with infinite capacity for intrigue and surprise. In 1913 everyone knew the Great Powers were ready for war as never before, but no one could have predicted the crazy string of events the following summer that finally caused the shooting to start. The world now is much as it was then—dominated by superpowers armed to the teeth and swinging uneasily between belligerence and détente, and filled with small states of uncertain allegiance nursing bitter grievances. The first step toward lessening the probability of nuclear war is admitting that it *can* happen.

But how might it start?

As we look at the world situation today and try to envision chains of events which might make a country consider using nuclear weapons, we see certain common elements—touchpoints—which suggest danger. First, one must acknowledge that the spheres of influence and interests of the two superpowers overlap in so many ways and in so many geographic areas that the chance of conflict is never distant. Whether it is over Olympic medals or Persian Gulf oil, the two sides often clash in what war-gamers call zero-sum situations—conflicts in which one side's gain is the other's loss. Both sides, aware of the danger, try to avoid open confrontation. They also try to control their allies, who have interests and ambitions of their own—not an easy task. "Hot spots"—areas of local conflict such as the Middle East, the Persian Gulf, Central America, Berlin, or Southeast Asia—abound. Taken together these two factors—zero-sum situations and hot spots—routinely result in crises, any one of which might escalate into nuclear war.

Most crises involving the superpowers are settled through careful diplomacy and without bloodshed. But the danger always exists that either side, through foolhardy commitment or lack of foresight, might paint itself into a corner, creating a "lose-lose, damned if you do, damned if you don't" situation. With its back to the wall, a great power may find itself tempted to use a nuclear weapon—perhaps only a small one at first—rather than accept the certain or probable loss of troops, resources, an ally, or even international prestige and power—the common currency of international politics.

In war, it is said, nothing is certain. Wars tend to begin in unpredictable ways, as the result of "causes" that might only ruffle the international waters in other circumstances. A *casus belli*—or cause of war—is an after-the-fact assessment of something that led to war, not something that *has* to result in war. What are such causes? How might a nuclear war occur?

The scenarios that follow attempt to shed light on this question. They do not pretend to predict the future; they only describe events of a sort that are common in today's world and *might* lead to war. Situations like those outlined here have all occurred at one time or another in the last thirty-seven years. The preliminary steps, or events much like them, can be expected to occur again. If someday the final steps are taken and war follows in fact, we shall, as always, be surprised.

The Scenarios

The various "moves" in a war-game scenario can be presented in almost any level of detail. They can be scratched out on the back of an envelope or involve huge computers and reams of printout. The war-gamers do both. Some people find them more credible with more detail; some like less.

This book opened with an Iran/Persian Gulf scenario for the start of World War III. Four more are presented in this chapter: one in the Middle East, one in Western Europe, one in the context of a new Cuban missile crisis, and one as a result of technical malfunction. The first—the Middle East scenario—is described in considerable detail. The others are more concise. If you don't like these, you can do your own. In fact, there will probably soon be a World War III board game like Monopoly. Call it Ground Zero.

A: THE MIDDLE EAST
The Arab-Israeli Situation Explodes

Days 1–4: The new Mubarak regime in Egypt is overthrown by Islamic extremists who immediately sign a friendship treaty with Libya's Qaddafi, offer Russia a naval base in return for arms, and bitterly disavow the Camp David accords.

Day 5: Israel announces a halt in its Camp David accords–mandated withdrawal from Sinai and puts military forces on alert.

Day 7: Palestinian terrorists based in Lebanon ambush a school bus in northern Israel, killing thirteen children.

Day 8: Israel retaliates with air attacks on PLO camps in Lebanon but loses eight planes to Russian-made Syrian surface-to-air missiles.

Day 10: The Israeli defense forces launch a major raid on Syrian military units stationed in southern Lebanon. While the United States urges moderation on all sides, the Soviet Union denounces Israel in the UN.

Days 11–12: Syrian and PLO forces put up an unexpectedly effective defense against Israeli raiders, wiping out an entire Israeli infantry company and destroying many Israeli tanks. Israel describes casualties as "no worse than expected" and launches deep penetration raids into northern Lebanon and Syria. Syria claims to have shot down forty-three Israeli planes; Israel insists it has lost only a few planes; informed sources in Tel Aviv concede the number is "about a dozen."

Day 13:   The Soviet Union announces it "will not tolerate further Israeli outrages" in the Middle East. The United States calls for a cease-fire in the UN. Qaddafi calls for a holy war against Israel and claims that Libya is armed with "a secret weapon of unusual destructive force."

Day 14:   Syria announces the downing of sixty-nine more Israeli aircraft. UN observers in southern Lebanon report large contingents of Israeli reinforcements crossing the frontier.

Day 15:   Jordan declares "all-out support of our Arab brothers." Egypt is reported to be mobilizing its armed forces.

Day 17:   Israel announces it has sunk a freighter carrying "replacement antiaircraft missiles" to Syria. Moscow denounces this "act of war on the high seas." Informed sources in Bonn confirm that the ship, of Liberian registry, was transporting Russian missile teams to Syria.

Day 18:   Damascus claims to have shot down 271 Israeli aircraft since the fighting began; Israeli sources admit to 35. Iraq announces it will join Qaddafi's holy war against Israel, using "any weapons necessary."

Days 19–21: Informed sources in Tel Aviv report the loss of an Israeli destroyer, sunk by a Libyan plane. The *New York Times* reports that the lost ship was a frigate, not a destroyer, and that it was sunk by the Syrians. The Tokyo *Asahi Shimbun* correspondent in Peking reports that *two* destroyers were sunk by a Soviet missile frigate and that China is alerting its forces in Sinkiang as a warning to the "hegemonists."

Day 22: Sources in the intelligence community in Washington report danger of full-scale naval combat between Russia and Israel. The president helicopters to Camp David, where he is to spend the weekend with his economic advisers reviewing the next year's federal budget.

Day 23: Moscow announces that one of its helicopter carriers in the eastern Mediterranean has been attacked by Israeli jets and warns that any further "acts of Zionist piracy" will be treated as "acts of war." The White House press secretary announces that the president has "a mild case of flu" and that the Camp David cabinet meeting has been canceled.

Day 25: Informed sources in London report "unusual activity" at Russian airfields in the Transcaucasus. The *New York Times* reports that all Polaris/Poseidon submarines at the Charleston Naval Base have put to sea.

Day 26: Damascus announces that two Israeli divisions have been "trapped" in the Bikal Valley of central Lebanon and that its "heroic Islamic missilemen" have driven Israeli planes from the skies.

Day 27: Moscow, Cairo, Tripoli, Damascus, and Baghdad announce a series of twenty-year pacts to "resist Zionist aggressors." Jordan's King Hussein says he is "assessing the situation."

Day 29: The Israeli ambassador to the UN announces that "Soviet-built aircraft flown

by Russian pilots" have raided the Israeli naval base at Eilat from the former
U.S. Wheelis Air Base in Libya.

Day 30: British Prime Minister Margaret
Thatcher and French President François
Mitterand jointly call for a cease-fire in
the region. Saudi Arabia announces that
it is halting oil shipments to the United
States and will do the same to any other
country supporting the Israelis. The
leaders of twelve Jewish organizations in
the United States call upon the president
to "save Israel from a second holocaust."

Day 31: Israeli troops retake the entire Sinai pen-
insula with little resistance from Egyp-
tian forces. Russia warns Israel against
"acts of war."

Day 32: The U.S. secretary of state resigns, citing "personal reasons." His replace-
ment, the president's national security
adviser, says that "the United States will
stand by its friends. This is no time for
another Munich." A *Washington Post*
columnist reports that after a shouting
match at a Camp David meeting, the
secretary of state, in fact, fired by
the president.

Day 34: "The CBS Evening News" reports that
a U.S. satellite has detected what appears to be "a small nuclear explosion"
in Libya. Washington, Moscow, Tel
Aviv, and other governments refuse to
comment on the report.

Day 35: A *London Times* correspondent in Peking writes that Chinese "military
officials report Israeli destruction of the

former Wheelis Air Base in Libya with a nuclear device in the ten-kiloton range."

Day 36: The editors of the *New York Times*, the London *Sunday Times*, the *Washington Post*, *Le Monde* (Paris), *Frankfurter Allgemeine Zeitung*, and other major newspapers in NATO member countries publish a common editorial calling for "patience, restraint, and calm deliberation at this uncertain moment."

Day 37: Villagers in southern Cyprus report a "great white light" to the south. The Reuters news agency reports that the aircraft carrier U.S.S. *Saratoga* has been "lost" in the Mediterranean.

Day 40: The United States and the Soviet Union jointly announce that a general cease-fire has "been imposed" in the Middle East and that Israel has agreed to withdrawal to its prewar positions.

Day 41: Jordan's King Hussein declares war on Israel and demands return of the West Bank and Jerusalem.

Day 42: American dead: 3,600 members of the crew of the U.S.S. *Saratoga* and support craft.
Israeli dead: 4,000.
Libyan dead: Unknown.
Russian dead: Moscow refuses to concede that any Russians have been killed.

B: THE CARIBBEAN
Russian Missiles in Cuba Again?

Background: After a delay of several years, Bonn has officially given the United States permission to begin deploying Pershing II ballistic missiles and Tomahawk ground-launched cruise missiles in West Germany. Denouncing this "naked attempt to achieve nuclear superiority," Russia has announced plans to accelerate deployment of SS-20 missiles. In response, the president of the U.S. has accused the Soviets of "nuclear blackmail," publicly instructed the secretary of defense to double the planned number of American missiles in Europe, and called for serious negotiations on the reduction of missile forces in the European theater. In the meantime, the chancellor of West Germany has lost a vote of confidence in parliament and announced new elections.

Day 1: The director of central intelligence tells the president's national security adviser that the CIA has "proof positive" that the Soviets are shipping ground-launched cruise missiles to Cuba.

Day 2: The president summons the Soviet ambassador to the White House and, citing the "proof positive" that the Soviets have broken the 1962 Cuban agreement, threatens "grave consequences" if the new missiles are not removed. The Soviet ambassador heatedly denies the charge.

Day 3: Moscow announces that Cuba is an integral part of "the socialist community of nations" and will be defended "by any means necessary." The CIA reports that an American reconnaissance satellite has abruptly stopped broadcasting. Five hundred thousand West Germans demonstrate in Bonn, calling for peace and the removal of "all nuclear weapons from German soil."

Day 4: The CIA reports passage of Soviet nuclear submarines through the Baltic Sea toward the North Sea.

Day 5: On national television, the president announces a quarantine of Cuba until the Soviet Union pledges to remove all "offensive weapons" from the island.

Day 6: Moscow denies the presence of nuclear weapons in Cuba and accuses the United States of "stirring up war fever" in order to justify an invasion of the island.

Day 7: The U.S. ambassador to the UN unveils aerial reconnaissance photographs of missile launching construction sites in Cuba and reports that "a source in the Cuban government" has confirmed the presence of missiles. The U.S. ambassadors to Britain, France, and West Germany privately inform the heads of government of those countries that the CIA's source is a military aide to the Cuban minister of defense.

Day 9: In a televised speech, Fidel Castro invites observers from three "nonaligned countries"—India, Algeria, and Libya—to inspect the "alleged sites." He then introduces a military aide to the defense minister, who confesses he has been fabricating "secrets" to sell to the CIA.

Day 11: The NATO commander-in-chief and two aides are assassinated in Brussels.

Day 12: India, Algeria, and Libya accept the invitation to send observers to Cuba.

Day 13: The U.S. secretary of defense insists that the quarantine of Cuba will be maintained until "a truly neutral observer" can visit the alleged missile sites. All road and rail traffic to West Berlin is halted by East German border guards checking papers.

Day 15: A poll by the West German magazine *Der Spiegel* shows that a Christian Democratic "peace candidate" will win the election by an overwhelming margin. Indian, Algerian, and Libyan observers report that a school and senior citizens' community center are under construction at the "alleged missile sites" in Cuba.

Day 16: On national television, the president insists the U.S. has proof of Soviet missiles in Cuba "from sources too secret to reveal." He calls on the Western allies to "hold firm." The prime minister of Britain, the president of France, and the chancellor of West Germany call on the U.S. president to "exercise patience and restraint at this difficult time." The mayor of West Berlin announces his support for the "peace candidate," asserting that "it is time to end the last war" and calling for a change in the city's status.

Day 17:   The U.S. secretary of defense announces, "The quarantine is in effect. If Soviet ships do not turn around, they will be halted by force."

Day 20:   The Soviet Union announces "routine military maneuvers" in Poland, East Germany, Czechoslovakia, and Bulgaria.

Day 21:   A U.S. aircraft carrier task force in the Caribbean approaches two Soviet freighters. The mayor of West Berlin accepts an East German offer of food and heating oil "to avert an imminent crisis." Moscow calls on the U.S. to "accept reality" and "end the quarantine joke."

Day 22:   The CIA tells the president that all U.S. reconnaissance satellites are silent. The president orders a full-scale alert.

Day 23:   The chief of naval operations announces that a Soviet freighter has been sunk. The commander of a U.S. carrier in the Caribbean reports his ship is under torpedo attack.

Day 24:   Moscow detonates a nuclear weapon 30,000 feet above NATO headquarters near Brussels. Windows are shattered throughout the city. Some roofs collapse.

Day 25:   Britain, France, and West Germany declare "a condition of temporary neutrality."

Day 26:   The U.S. launches a single Minuteman III missile with three warheads toward a Soviet submarine base on the Baltic Sea.

Day 27:   Russia launches preemptive counter-
                  force strikes against U.S. ICBM sites
                  and immediately calls for a cessation of
                  hostilities. The United States responds
                  immediately with an attack on Soviet
                  submarine and bomber bases, ICBM and
                  IRBM silos, and Soviet troop concentra-
                  tions on the Chinese border.

Day 28:   Surviving Soviet missiles, including sev-
                  eral hundred Cuba-based cruise missiles,
                  respond with an all-out nuclear attack on
                  population and industrial centers of the
                  United States, Western Europe, and
                  China.

Day 29:   The United States responds with a strike
                  against Soviet and Eastern bloc popula-
                  tion and industrial centers.

Day 30:   American dead: 140 million.
                  Soviet dead: 120 million.
                  European dead: 120 million.
                  Chinese dead: 100 million.

C: EUROPE
A Tale of Two Germanys

Background: As the result of broad grass-roots sup-
                  port, nuclear disarmament in West Ger-
                  many became by far the major issue at
                  the April 1982 meeting of the Social
                  Democratic Party (SPD) and in the sub-
                  sequent election campaign. The United
                  States attributed this development to
                  "naked Soviet intervention" in West
                  German affairs and insisted that U.S.
                  forces would not "desert Europe, or

leave it defenseless." This "high-handed" U.S. reaction outraged the Germans, and many left-wing SPD candidates who campaigned on a platform of European nuclear disarmament were elected to the West German parliament.

Day 1: A proposal to withdraw militarily from NATO, as France had done in the mid-1960s, is introduced into the new West German Bundestag but fails by a narrow margin. The Bundestag does, however, vote to schedule a gradual removal of nuclear weapons from West German soil and a simultaneous increase in the nation's own conventional forces.

Day 10: East German unions, which have defied their government to form a "Unity" movement modeled on Poland's Solidarity Union and establish contact with West German unions, announce plans for a "German Solidarity Day."

Day 20: Reunification is proposed in the West German parliament under the slogan "One Germany, free from terror."

Days 30–40: The United States and the Soviet Union independently warn "all peace-loving Germans" that reunification is out of the question. Nevertheless, massive demonstrations in both countries are held in support of the proposal for German Solidarity Day.

Day 45: The Soviet Union declares that further demonstrations in support of German reunification will have "dire consequences."

Day 48: A huge crowd at a Unity demonstration

in Berlin throws stones at the Soviet Embassy.

Days 50–55: Soviet military forces in East Germany leave their garrisons and enter major East German cities. The Soviet Union declares that it is reassuming responsibility for East German security. East German army units join local Unity groups and other citizenry in massive resistance. West Germany secretly begins sending war matériel across the border.

Days 55–60: Soviet troops and tanks massacre East German civilians. Bonn advises the United States of its intent to send troops into East Germany.

Days 60–62: The United States warns Bonn that its plans could provoke Soviet use of nuclear weapons. Other European NATO countries refuse to lend their support to West Germany. Six West German divisions cross the border and engage Soviet forces.

Days 62–70: Russia orders general mobilization and floods troops into East Germany. The United States warns Russia not to cross the West German border but begins withdrawal of all U.S. forces to positions in France, Belgium, and the Netherlands.

Day 72: U.S. military intelligence reports signs of Soviets making preparations for a nuclear strike, presumably against West Germany. The United States informs NATO allies of this threat and simultaneously warns the Soviet Union that a nuclear attack on any NATO nation will result in U.S. retaliation against the Soviet heartland.

Day 75: Moscow declares that any nuclear weapons directed at Soviet forces will be considered a full-scale attack by the United States and will be "responded to accordingly." Soviet troops cross into West Germany at a dozen points.

Day 80: Major elements of German forces retreat into France.

Day 81: Soviets ignore French warning not to enter French territory, and pursue West German forces into Alsace, engaging U.S. and French forces.

Day 82: France uses a small (one-kiloton) neutron bomb on Soviet troop concentrations in West Germany.

Day 83: The Soviets respond with a nuclear attack on several dozen military targets in France, Belgium, Holland, and northern Italy. Moscow warns the United States not to become involved. The British and French launch a portion of their submarine-based missile forces—about thirty SLBMs—against military targets in the western part of the Soviet Union, warning the Soviets that any further nuclear strikes on Western Europe will lead to an attack on Soviet cities.

Day 85: The United States calls for "a cease-fire in place." The Soviet Union accepts.

Day 86: American dead: 300,000 troops in Europe.
European dead: 2,000,000.
Soviet dead: 500,000 troops and civilians.

D: THE PERILS OF "LAUNCH ON WARNING"

Background: In the early 1980s, the United States secretly adopted plans to develop a "counterforce" capability against Soviet ICBMs; i.e., the ability to target and destroy Soviet ICBM missiles in their hardened silos, through the deployment of several hundred M-X and Trident II missiles. Deducing the U.S. strategy from congressional testimony and Pentagon procurement plans, the Soviets have adopted a "launch on warning" or "launch on attack" posture; i.e., they will launch their missiles as soon as they can confirm a U.S. attack against them, rather than lose the missiles in their silos.

Meanwhile, relations between the United States and the Soviet Union have deteriorated on all fronts. The perceived Russian role in the increasingly repressive domestic actions of Eastern Europe governments has resulted in severe U.S. economic and diplomatic sanctions. Movement of additional Syrian "peace-keeping" forces into Lebanon has precipitated Israeli mobilization and recently led the U.S. ambassador to the UN to refer to the Soviet government as "malevolent pupeteers."

Day 1: At 5:00 A.M. (Moscow time) on December 25, Soviet reconnaissance satellites indicate that the United States has launched the majority of its ICBMs against the Soviet Union. Computer analysis confirms that a major strike is under way. The Soviet president is awakened by his military aide, hurriedly wrapped in a fur robe, and rushed through the bitter Moscow cold to a waiting helicopter. A colonel in the rocket forces tells the president of the warning—not nine minutes old—and hands him a telephone that is connected to the chief of staff of Soviet forces. The chief of staff says at least a thousand Soviet ICBMs are threatened and recommends that Soviet missiles be launched immediately.

Still barely awake, the Soviet premier stares down at his bare feet, unprotected from the cold metal of the helicopter floor. After a long pause, he looks up at the military aide who had bundled him into the helicopter and asks: "Dimitri, you said the new warning system had not yet been adequately tested. Could this be a computer malfunction, or is it the real thing?"

"Mr. Premier," he answers, "I don't know. The system is at least 95 percent reliable, but it's 6:00 P.M. Washington time, and it's hard to believe the Americans would launch an attack on Christmas Eve. Still, George Washington once attacked the Hessians on Christmas Eve during the American Revolution, so it's not without precedent."

"Dimitri, you spent three years at our embassy in Washington. You know the Americans, including the president, better than I. I am old and tired and cold, and I will die soon, regardless of what decision I make here tonight. The future

of Russia is your future, not mine, so I
will leave it to you. Do I launch or not?
You decide."

Day 2:   American dead: None. Or perhaps 140
million.

PART III

More than You'll Ever Want to Know: The Consequences of Nuclear War

9

The Good News Is You Will Be Killed Instantly: The Immediate Effects of Nuclear War

Somewhere in the Soviet Union, probably at a military base just outside Moscow, a young officer sits at a desk with a plastic template, carefully drawing circles on a large-scale map of the United States. This officer—call him Ivan the Targeteer—wields with his template more destructive power than the eighteenth-century czar Ivan the Terrible ever dreamed of. He is deciding who lives and who dies in a nation of 240 million people—the United States. A fable? Not really, for this is essentially how Soviet targeting of the United States is done.

Not surprisingly, in a similar room at Strategic Air Command headquarters near Omaha, Nebraska, a young U.S. officer performs the same task, using a map of the Soviet Union. The American—call him Kilroy—is probably aided by a vast computer. But, in the end, the job and the way it's done are still the same—decide what you want to destroy, and then position the circles representing the lethal radii for various nuclear weapons so as to maximize the damage. Ivan and Kilroy are targeteers.

The Targeted

By now you're probably wondering how Ivan the Targeteer decides where to place his little circles—and

whether you are inside one of them. It's a grim form of
Russian roulette—instead of one chamber being
loaded, only one is empty. As the titles of this chapter
and the next imply, you're probably not sure whether
"the winners" are inside or outside the circles.

Ivan and Kilroy both lock up their maps at night so
the other side can't find out with precision just where
the circles are. But both sides can make a pretty good
guess. The procedure is simple. Take the biblical rule
"Do unto others as you would have them do unto
you" and turn it inside out. We guess that the Soviets
will do unto us as we plan to do unto them. How, then,
does Kilroy the Targeteer choose his circles?

Inside Kilroy's Circles: Targeting the Soviet Union

In the United States, the plan for targeting the
Soviet Union is called the Single Integrated Operational Plan, or, in common parlance, the SIOP (pronounced "sigh-OP"). As will be discussed in Chapter
12, the plan is not for a single "burp" or "spasm" that
would send thousands of nuclear weapons toward the
Soviet Union, although very early versions of the plan
called for just such attacks. Rather, the SIOP offers a
series of choices—more than one but less than one
hundred—that give the president substantial flexibility
in the use of nuclear weapons. Kilroy prepares a
separate map of the Soviet Union for each choice or
option. The detailed plans are, of course, highly
classified, but the rough outlines of some of them have
been revealed over the years in official statements by
the president, military leaders, and officials of the
Defense Department. Two of the most important are:

   —A U.S. "first-strike" option in which most of the
   ten thousand nuclear weapons in the U.S. strategic arsenal would be launched in a preemptive
   strike against the Soviet Union—to get them be-

fore they get us. This is sometimes referred to as a "damage-limiting" strategy.

—A U.S. "second-strike" option in which most of the seven thousand* nuclear weapons which would survive a Soviet first strike would be launched in retaliation.

In either case, when Kilroy the Targeteer draws his circles on a map of the Soviet Union, his objective is to do the greatest possible damage to three categories of Soviet targets: industry, leadership, and military forces.

Note that Kilroy's three target categories do not include people. In the late 1940s and early 1950s, when the bombs were few and cumbersome, the Strategic Air Command planned to drop most of them on Russian cities. With so many warheads to work with now, Kilroy can pick his targets with greater care, but the effect is pretty much the same. The circles which Kilroy draws around factories and power plants are almost indistinguishable from those which he would draw if he were simply trying to kill as many people as possible. The simple truth is that Russians, like Americans, live where the jobs are. The target categories are a sort of grim charade in which consciences are eased by the argument that we do not seek to kill people, just buildings and machines. It's probably easier on Kilroy.

Soviet leadership targets include the Kremlin and underground bunkers outside Moscow and other major cities where the Soviet leadership would probably hole up. Obviously, it would not be wise to hang around if there were an international crisis and you saw a fleet of large black Volga limousines disappear-

---

*The number of surviving weapons would depend on the alert status of U.S. forces. In a crisis, the most likely situation in which a nuclear war would start, most submarines would be at sea and most bombers would be on alert, so that about seven thousand weapons would survive. In a "bolt-from-the-blue" attack, a lower number (about six thousand) would survive.

ing into a tunnel in the Ural mountains. Tunnels are one of the things reconnaissance satellites are good at finding. A 170-kiloton Minuteman warhead could easily be knocking on the tunnel door within a matter of hours.

Military targets include missile silos, bomber bases, supply depots, military district headquarters, nuclear weapons storage sites, and the offices where Ivan and his colleagues are plotting *their* circles. Many of these are also near cities, so the U.S. aversion to targeting people is essentially meaningless. Whether by accident or design, people are inside the circles. It is, as they say, all the same in the end.

A rough breakdown of Kilroy's circles for U.S. attacks on the Soviet Union is shown in Table 9.1.

Whether we attack first or second, the results would be much the same. U.S. warheads would destroy over 70 percent of Soviet military forces, over 90 percent of key industries (steel, aircraft, tanks, trucks, power, etc.), over 70 percent of overall industrial capacity, and all Soviet cities with a population over twenty-five thousand or so.

TABLE 9.1
Distribution of U.S. Nuclear Warheads
on Soviet Targets

	U.S. 1st Strike	U.S. 2nd Strike
ICBM silos	3,000	1,500
Other military targets	2,500	2,500
Leadership	500	500
Industry	1,000	1,000
Held in reserve	3,000	4,500
Total	10,000	7,000*

*Approximately 3,000 U.S. nuclear warheads on missiles and bombers would be destroyed by a Soviet first strike. Most of these would be on ICBMs in silos.

About 120 million people—children, brothers, sisters, moms, dads, grandfathers, and grandmothers—would be killed instantly or die within a few weeks from radiation and other injuries.

Inside Ivan's Circles: Targeting the United States

As is indicated above, we think that Ivan's targeting of the United States would closely follow Kilroy's approach to targeting the Soviet Union. This is a case in which there is only one way to skin a cat. Today the Soviet Union has about seven thousand nuclear warheads which could be used in a first strike against targets in the United States. If the United States were to launch a first strike against the Soviet Union—which seems unlikely to us, perhaps, but not to them—about six thousand Soviet warheads would survive and could be used in a second strike against the United States. The breakdown of how these warheads might be distributed between various target categories is shown in Table 9.2.

Attacks such as these would destroy virtually all of our military forces except for 10 to 20 percent of our ICBMs, our submarines at sea, those few surface ships

TABLE 9.2
Distribution of Soviet Nuclear Warheads on U.S. Targets

	Soviet 1st Strike	Soviet 2nd Strike
ICBM silos	2,000	1,500
Other military targets	2,000	1,000
Cities	1,000	1,000
Held in reserve	3,000	2,500
Total	7,000	6,000

which escape Soviet nuclear-armed cruise missiles
and torpedoes, and those bombers which get off the
ground and head toward the Soviet Union to retaliate.
Over 80 percent of U.S. industry—including almost all
basic industry—would be destroyed.

About 140 million Americans—children, brothers,
sisters, moms, dads, grandfathers, and grandmothers—would be killed instantly or die within a few
weeks from radiation and other injuries.

Ivan, Kilroy, and Europe

While it is not treated in detail in this book, Europe
would almost certainly be involved in any nuclear war
between the United States and the Soviet Union. Ivan
has also drawn many circles on a map of Western
Europe, and Kilroy has done the same for Eastern
European countries such as Poland and Czechoslovakia.

In an all-out nuclear war the immediate death toll in
Europe would be about 120 million people.

Would My City Be Attacked?

Probably. Table 9.3 summarizes the impact of a
Soviet attack on U.S. cities using a thousand one-
megaton weapons—a good guess (see Table 9.2) at the
number of weapons the Soviets would commit to city
attacks.

You may from time to time see other nuclear
weapon "laydowns" (that's the technical term) which
show more or fewer weapons aimed at the larger U.S.
cities—perhaps as many as forty or as few as twelve at
New York City. It wouldn't make much difference if
nuclear war really happened. You may also see maps
of your city with concentric "overpressure" circles
showing what a single one-megaton weapon would do.
Some residents of posh suburbs on the outskirts of big
cities take heart from these maps, thinking their com-

munities will be only lightly damaged. That's an illusion. As shown in Table 9.3, your "fair share" will certainly be several one-megaton weapons. Note that even cities of only ten thousand people are likely to be attacked. Why? Because many contain factories, light industry, and skilled workers who could help the U.S. recover more quickly than the Soviet Union from a nuclear war.

It's awesome and it's grim, but this is the true story of nuclear war and what's in it for you.

A Walk Away from Ground Zero—in Detroit

To understand what a nuclear explosion actually does to a city, it is helpful to imagine an attack on a typical urban target—say, Detroit, Michigan. (The Congressional Office of Technology Assessment picked Detroit for its description of the effects of a nuclear attack on a city—from which this material is drawn.)

Suppose a one-megaton bomb was detonated at ground level in the middle of downtown Detroit. (See Figure 9.1.) Assuming that the explosion occurred at a time when most people were in their homes, this is what you would see.

Starting at the point of detonation, you would find yourself in a huge crater about a thousand feet wide and two hundred feet deep. As you left the crater—no easy task, as the rim of accumulated debris would rise dozens of feet above the normal level of the ground—the first recognizable landmarks would be a few massive concrete bridge abutments and building foundations. You would not find any significant standing structures until you had climbed your way 1.7 miles over layers of debris piled as high as ten or twenty feet. At the outer perimeter of this area, blast overpressure from the bomb would have been at least 12 pounds per square inch (psi) above normal atmospheric pressure. Most important, of the approxi-

TABLE 9.3
Consequences of a Soviet Attack on U.S. Cities: One-Megaton Weapons

Metropolitan Area	Population (Millions)	Weapons Used	Deaths (Millions)	Deaths plus Injuries (Millions)
New York	16.3	18	12.9	15.9
Los Angeles	8.7	13	6.9	8.3
Chicago	6.7	11	5.0	6.3
Philadelphia	4.6	10	3.6	4.3
Detroit	3.9	8	3.1	3.7
San Francisco	3.6	7	2.8	3.4
Boston	2.9	6	2.0	2.6
Washington, D.C.	2.6	5	1.9	2.4
Miami	2.3	5	1.6	2.0
Dallas	2.1	5	1.3	1.8
Cleveland	1.9	5	1.1	1.7
Houston	1.8	5	1.1	1.7
St. Louis	1.8	5	1.1	1.6

Pittsburgh	1.7	4	1.0	1.5
Minneapolis	1.6	4	1.0	1.4
Baltimore	1.5	3	.9	1.3
Subtotal	64.0	103	48.3	59.5
All other U.S. urban areas with population over 25,000.	68.0	627	55.0	64.0
Subtotal	132.0	730	103.3	123.6
All other U.S. urban areas with population over about 10,000	46.0	270	37.2	46.0
TOTAL	188.0	1000	140.5	169.5

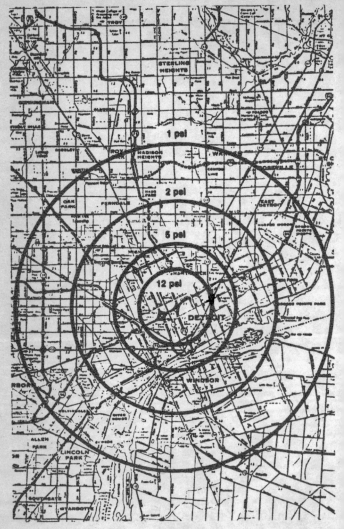

FIGURE 9.1
A One-Megaton Nuclear Weapon on Detroit

mately seventy thousand people inside the 12-psi range during nonworking hours, there would be virtually no survivors.

As you worked your way through into the second (5-psi) circle, you would find all homes blasted flat. Only basements and foundations would survive more or less intact. Although most heavy industrial plants in the inner part of the circle would be destroyed, some industry on the outer periphery of the 5-psi range would remain in usable condition. About half of this area's nighttime population of two hundred fifty thousand would be dead, and most of the remainder would have sustained injuries. Most of the fatalities would have occurred from collapsing buildings, flying debris, fire, and the like.

When you reached the third (2-psi) circle, most buildings would be partially destroyed. Many automobiles in this area would be in working condition, but their usefulness would be limited by the debris that cluttered the streets. Twenty thousand of the four hundred thousand people in this area would be dead, and nearly two hundred thousand would be injured. In addition, fires would pose a severe threat in the 2-psi range, since they start and spread more easily in partially damaged areas littered with kindling material than in areas smashed flat.

The damage in the outer (1-psi) range would be light in comparison to the inner areas. For the first time you would find something that still looked like a city. Commercial structures and homes would have sustained only minor damage. Twenty-five percent of the population in this area would be injured and a few percent—still in the thousands, of course—would be dead.

Following the initial physical destruction, less direct effects of the blast would begin to take their toll. For example, the task of treating the half million injured survivors would pose a staggering burden. Of the eighteen thousand hospital beds in the Detroit area, about 55 percent—those located inside the 5-psi circle—would be destroyed immediately. The additional 15 percent in the 2-psi range would be heavily damaged, leaving only about five thousand beds for the entire Detroit metropolitan area—approximately one bed for every hundred victims. Even if transportation could be found to take victims to hospitals in other parts of the state, there would be little point in moving them. Most of the other cities would have been attacked, too. The brutal fact is that most victims would get no treatment. Even more striking is the fact that although there would be tens of thousands of severe burn victims from the Detroit explosion, almost no specialized burn treatment would be available. (There are fewer than one hundred specialized burn centers with a total of only two thousand beds in the United States, and almost all of them are in major cities.) The lack of food, medicine, shelter, and clean water would increase the danger of infection or disease. In addition, many of Detroit's doctors and nurses would be dead or injured themselves.

Another effect of the nuclear explosion would be the almost total loss of utilities. Major disruptions of electrical service would also occur in areas of partial damage due to the collapse of buildings and toppling of trees on power lines. Water and gas distribution, even if the lines were structurally intact, would be stopped immediately because of loss of pressure caused by loss of electrical power to water and gas pumps.

Bad as the initial blast would be, the one which followed might be even worse. Thermal radiation—which is just another word for heat—would ignite kindling materials such as leaves, newspapers, and wood from shattered houses. Blast damage to furnaces, gas lines, or electrical circuits would cause additional fires where fuel was plentiful. It is also possible that a number of these fires could combine into a mass fire which would further threaten survivors of the initial blast. These mass fires could be either fire storms, in which violent inrushing winds would build extremely high temperatures while preventing the fire from spreading outward, or conflagrations, in which the fire spreads outward according to local geography, the speed and direction of the wind, and types of building construction. Although the severity of fire is difficult to determine in advance, there is little doubt that Detroit would burn.

The above description of the destruction of one of America's premier cities by a single one-megaton weapon is sobering—and optimistic. The fact is, as shown in Table 9.3, Detroit would not be attacked by a single one-megaton weapon but by many such weapons. Table 9.3 allocates eight; it could be five, it might be ten. In any case, the damage to the Detroit metropolitan area would be complete. Detroit would be gone, and it would be decades if not centuries before anyone would brave the radioactivity to return.

What Would You Do?

The *questions* of nuclear war start to become personal when the *effects* of such a war become personal. How would you react if your family were killed in a nuclear attack? Would you know when you could go outside without exposing yourself to lethal doses of radiation or active fallout? How would you treat a person who begged you for food if you didn't have enough for yourself? Could you live without water, heat, and light? Could you face the task of rebuilding? What would you tell friends who said they wished they had died right away? These questions would begin at the moment of detonation, and the questions would get harder with every passing hour for a long time to come.

This has been the "good news" chapter. The next chapter describes the postwar world.

10

The Bad News Is You Might Survive:
The Aftermath of a Nuclear Exchange

War happens to people, not "countries." War touches
the lives of individuals, killing some, injuring others,
bringing trauma and grief to those who have lost
homes and loved ones. Nuclear war would be much
the same, although it would have some macabre additional effects of its own. Nobody can comprehend the
totality of the horror of a major nuclear war. But you
can imagine how it might affect you. Just look around
at your neighborhood, your environment, your
friends, and your family—and then start taking them
away: your house, your car, the trees in your yard, the
people next door, the library in town, the evening
news on television, the bus to work, the supermarket,
the phone calls to parents at Christmas. A major
nuclear war would strip all that is familiar from your
life. None of the relationships so familiar to you, and
especially the "people" relationships of family and
friends, would ever be the same again.

Imagine that you were one of the "lucky" ones—
one of the survivors. What would your life be like?
Water and electricity would be cut immediately and
indefinitely. If the attack came in winter, any shelter
you could find would get cold quickly and stay cold.
Communications would be confined to a small number
of mobile radio systems. You wouldn't know what was

happening. How many cities were hit? Was the president alive? What about relatives living elsewhere—had they survived? What about the Russians—had they been hit, too? How did the war start? Was it over, or would there soon be more bombs? You might *never* learn the answers to many of these questions.

If you were injured you would hurt, and you would probably hurt until you got better or died. The few surviving medical facilities would be overwhelmed by the massive numbers of injured. Most would never see a doctor and would receive no medication—not even an aspirin.

The world as you know it would be gone. The world which followed would be different; no one can say exactly how. Most policemen, firemen, and government officials would be dead or injured. Banks and bank records would be gone. Paper money would be worthless. All the things people worry about—paying the mortgage, sending the kids to college, visiting parents, building a business—would come to a halt for months at best, most likely for years, perhaps forever.

If you had anything at all—a few cans of food, a blanket, a warm coat for your child—somebody stronger might come and take it from you. You might even find yourself committing acts you would have once found deplorable in order to survive.

You would wonder what was falling from the sky.

Every day for weeks you would see people die.

Fallout: A Hard Rain's A-Gonna Fall

One distinctive element of post-*nuclear*-war world would be fallout.

When a nuclear weapon is detonated at or near ground level, the so-called fireball at the center of the explosion picks up soil and dirt from the ground. Some of this material—thousands of tons of it, in the case of big bombs—is converted to very fine dust particles and carried to high altitudes in the mushroom cloud.

These dust particles, which contain radioactive material from the nuclear explosion, then fall back to earth downwind from the point of the explosion. It is these radioactive particles which are called fallout. There are many different kinds of radioactive material in fallout. Some is dangerous for only a few days. Some remains lethal for years.

Radioactive fallout is in effect a kind of poison that can be absorbed through the skin, breathed in, or eaten. It is accumulative, which means that it collects in the body. When the accumulated dose rises above a certain level, the result is "radiation sickness," a disease that attacks the bone marrow and other parts of the body. The first symptoms are vomiting and diarrhea, followed by anemia, loss of hair, possible skin sores, increased susceptibility to infection, and finally—in the worst cases—death. Thousands of people died of radiation sickness after the explosions at Hiroshima and Nagasaki.

Some forms of fallout can be seen as a fine film of dust, but most are invisible. Radioactivity cannot be seen, smelled, tasted, or felt. Only special instruments can detect its presence. People can protect themselves from fallout by staying indoors for two weeks or more after a nuclear explosion. Even an ordinary frame house provides much protection. A basement is better; an underground shelter with a thick covering of earth and an air-filtration system is best of all. But radiation also contaminates food and water, and most survivors of a nuclear explosion would have no way of knowing whether what they were eating and drinking was safe—if they could get anything to eat and drink at all.

The map in Figure 10.1 depicts the radioactive fallout which will result from a general nuclear war in which the Soviet Union attacks American military and industrial targets with three thousand nuclear weapons. The shaded portions of the map represent those areas within which any exposed individual

FIGURE 10.1
Areas Covered by 100 REMs or More

would suffer serious injury.* Approximately 75 percent of the rural population of the United States, and virtually *all* of the urban population, is within the shaded areas. The 100-rem dose upon which the map is based is not always fatal, but it does have long-term effects. The main one is substantial increase in the risk of cancer.

Before you go running for southern Oregon or northern Minnesota, if the Soviet Union wished to deliberately cover all of the United States with a dangerous level of fallout, a few hundred additional well-placed nuclear weapons could probably achieve this goal. In that case, all of the map in Figure 10.1 would be shaded.

---

*In technical terms, the shaded areas represent exposure to 100 rems of radiation. A rem is a standard measure of radiation exposure which measures the amount of biological damage done by various types of radiation.

The Postwar World: A Clouded Image

The summary of the postwar world given above is sketchy and grim. If we tried to predict precisely what the world would be like using the most sophisticated computers and the most respected sociologists, economists, businessmen, and political scientists, we probably couldn't do much better. In the early 1970s the Pentagon attempted exactly that sort of analysis in a study called PONAST (Post Nuclear Attack Study). After the expenditure of millions of dollars and months of effort, the study was in effect thrown out. No one could say what to expect, because no one had been through anything like it.

The simple fact is that we really have very little idea what the postwar world would be like—just that it would be horrible. It is often said that "the living would envy the dead." To human beings, for whom life is so precious, such a statement seems inconceivable. Yet most Americans, when faced with the choice, say that they would prefer to die and die quickly.

Through a Glass Darkly: A Speculative Portrait of One Corner of the Postwar World

Where computers fail, human intelligence and imagination may succeed. If we cannot predict precisely what the world would be like after a nuclear war, we *can* piece together the kinds of events likely to transpire at the edge of a nuclear battlefield.

What follows is a fictionalized account of what might occur in a small American city remote from any strategic target in the aftermath of a full-scale nuclear attack on the United States. It is not fiction in the sense of being particularly fanciful. Rather, it has been constructed from a variety of things that we *do* know something about. We can predict the physical effects of a distant nuclear explosion on human bodies and the surface and atmosphere of the earth. We know from experience with natural disasters what happens when the economic, political, social, and utility systems of a complex society are temporarily disrupted or destroyed. We have seen at first hand what becomes of civility when people must compete for basic necessities in order to survive. In the light of these bodies of information, what is presented here might best be termed educated fiction—a straightforward picture of a community struggling to resurrect itself in the wake of the ultimate convulsion.

CHARLOTTESVILLE*

At first it seemed like a miracle. No fireball had seared the city, no blast wave had crumbled buildings and buried the inhabitants, no dark mushroom cloud had spread over the sky. Much of the country had been devastated by massive nuclear attack, but the small, gracious city of Charlottesville, Virginia, had escaped unharmed.

The nuclear attack on the nation did not come as a complete surprise. For some weeks there had been a mounting anxiety as the media reported deteriorating relations between the superpowers. As a consequence, spontaneous evacuation, without official sanction or direction, grew and spread. A week before the attack, there were no free hotel or motel rooms in Charlottesville and surrounding Albemarle County.

At the sound of the sirens and the emergency radio alerts, most of the ninety thousand residents of Charlottesville and Albemarle County (and the ap-

*This scenario is a condensed and edited version of one prepared by an author, Nan Randall, and originally published by the Office of Technology Assessment (OTA), Congress of the United States, in *The Effects of Nuclear War*, pp. 124–138. OTA commissioned this work of fiction in an effort to provide a more concrete understanding of the situation which survivors of a nuclear war would face. It presents one among many possibilities, and in particular it does not consider the situation if martial law were imposed or if the social fabric disintegrated into anarchy.

proximately thirty thousand refugees) hurried to shelter. Fortunately, Charlottesville had a surplus of shelter space for its own population, though the refugees easily took up the slack. Carrying a few personal effects, blankets, cans and bottles of food, and transistor radios, they converged in a quiet if unordered mass. For most people, the obvious emotional crises—grief at leaving behind a pet, anxiety at being unable to locate a family member or relative—were suppressed by the overwhelming fear of the impending attack.

Two and one half hours after the warnings had sounded, the nuclear engineering staff from the university picked up the first fallout. Starting at a moderate level of about 40 rems an hour—a cumulative dose of 450 rems received in a one-week period would be fatal to one half of those exposed—the intensity rose to 50 rems before starting the decline to a level of about four-tenths of a rem an hour after two weeks. (The total dose in the first four days was 2,000 rems, which killed those who refused to believe shelter was necessary, and increased the risk of eventually dying of cancer for those who were properly sheltered.) For the immediate period, it was essential to stay as protected as possible.

For the time being, the food stocks brought to the shelters were adequate if not appetizing. The only problem was the water supply, which, though it kept running because of its gravity system, was contaminated with Iodine 131. Potassium iodide pills, which were available in some shelters, provided protection; elsewhere people drank bottled water, or as little water as possible.

Three days after the attacks, the next large influx of refugees poured into Charlottesville, many of them suffering with the early symptoms of radiation sickness. They had been caught poorly sheltered or too close to the nuclear targets themselves.

(Some time later it was learned that more than 4,000 megatons [Mt] had destroyed military and industrial targets, killing close to 100 million people in the United States. The U.S. counterattack on the Soviet Union had had a similar devastating effect. Destruction ranged from the large industrial centers on the coasts and Great Lakes to small farming communities that had the misfortune to be close to the great missile silos and military bases.)

A few of the refugees showed the effects of blast and fire, bringing home to Charlottesville the tangible evidence of the war's destruction. Some refugees had driven, while others had hitchhiked or even walked to reach what they hoped was safety and medical help. On the way, many were forced to abandon those who were too weak to continue.

Refugees continued to arrive even while the fallout levels were too high for anyone to be out in the open for any length of time. The carefully laid plans of the University of Virginia Emergency Room, devised for the possibility of peacetime accidents, were hurriedly modified. No longer was the careful showering and decontaminating of victims possible with the single shower and uncertain water pressure. Instead, patients were stripped of their clothes and issued hospital gowns. With no time for studied decision, doctors segregated the very sick from the moderately sick— the latter to be treated, the former given medication and allowed to die. When the hospitals were full, the injured and ailing refugees could not be accommodated.

After being turned away, the sick had no specific destination. Hundreds still clustered around the middle of town near the two major hospitals, taking shelter in the houses abandoned by local residents several days before. With minimal protection from fallout and no medical treatment for other trauma, many died, their bodies left unburied for several weeks.

The combined populations of Charlottesville and

Albemarle County rose to one hundred fifty thousand—
including sixty thousand refugees—in the seven days
after the nuclear attack. Slowly, hostility and resentment wedged a gap beween residents and refugees who
attempted to join the group shelters. The refugees, still
dazed from their experience, believed that they had
priority rights after all they had suffered. The local
residents viewed the outsiders as a threat to their own
survival, particularly as the extent of the war damage
was becoming evident.

Electricity was restored, partially, some two weeks
after the attack. From then on, limited electricity use
was permitted for a few hours a day.

During the third week after the attacks, a new
rationing system was implemented. Individual
identification cards were issued to every man, woman,
and child. Food was distributed at centralized points.
Those without ID cards were unable to get their ration
of flour, powdered milk, and lard—and the processing
of cards could take three or more days.

The radioactivity level continued to drop (after two
weeks it was 0.4 rem per hour), and it was "safe" to go
outdoors. However, the resulting doses, though too
low to cause immediate illness or death, posed a
long-term health hazard. The authorities, while recognizing that everybody would receive many times the
prewar "safe dose," tried to reduce the hazards by
urging people to stay inside as much as possible when
not picking up food rations at the distribution centers.

Three weeks after the nuclear attack, almost all the
Charlottesville and Albemarle County residents had
returned to their homes. Those few whose homes had
been either occupied by squatters or destroyed by fire
easily found some alternate housing with the government's help.

This left the refugees. Though the drop in fallout
intensity allowed the refugees to move out of basements and interior halls, they still were forced to live a

version of camp life. They spent their endless empty hours waiting in lines for food, for a chance to use the bathrooms (which at least functioned now), for a chance to talk to authorities.

The city manager and the emergency government attempted to solve the refugee housing problem by billeting refugees in private homes. At first they asked for volunteers, but they got few. The authorities then announced that any house with fewer than two people per room would be assigned a refugee family. Resistance to this order was strong, and outright defiance was common, particularly in the outlying areas where it was hard to check. Families would pretend to comply and then simply force the refugees out as soon as the authorities had left. The refugees would struggle back to town or take up residence in barns or garages.

By now the emergency government recognized that the need for food was going to be acute. Without power for refrigeration, much food had spoiled; stocks of nonperishable foods were mostly exhausted. As the shortages became clear, the price of food skyrocketed.

The first of the deaths from radiation had occurred ten days after the attacks, and the number grew steadily. By now it was not uncommon to see mass funerals several times a day. The terminally ill were not cared for by the hospitals—there were too many, and there was nothing that could be done for them, anyway—so it was up to their families to do what they could. Fortunately, there were still ample supplies of morphine, and it was rumored that college students had donated marijuana. The city set aside several locations on the outskirts of town for mass graves.

The supply of drugs on hand at the hospitals was dwindling fast. The penicillin manufactured fairly easily in the laboratories at the university had to be administered with large veterinary hypodermics, as the homemade mix was too coarse for the small disposable hypos that most doctors stocked. There was a considerable shortage of needles. Other medications

NUCLEAR WAR

were in such short supply that many patients with chronic illnesses such as heart disease, kidney failure, respiratory problems, hypertension, and diabetes died within a few weeks.

Food riots broke out when the first large shipment of grain arrived five weeks after the attack. Three large tractor-trailers had pulled into the parking lot of the Citizens Commonwealth Building quite unexpectedly, the word of their arrival somehow misplaced between the Agriculture Department dispatchers and the local authorities. The trucks were greeted with cheers until the residents of Charlottesville discovered that they had been shipped raw grain rather than flour.

With only a fraction of the population knowing what to do with raw grain, a number of angry citizens broke open the sacks and scattered wheat through the parking lot. They in turn were set upon by those who wanted to conserve as much as possible. The local public safety forces waded into the melee with nightsticks and tear gas.

From this time on, it was almost impossible for the local authorities, not to mention the state and federal governments, to convince everyone they were getting a fair share. People in one section of town would watch suspiciously as delivery trucks passed them by and headed somewhere else. Blacks distrusted whites, the poor distrusted the rich, and everyone distrusted the refugees as "outsiders."

Psychologically, the population seemed to be in a quiet holding pattern. Many of the refugees had survived experiences that would mark them for years. The memories of fire, collapsing buildings, and screaming, trapped people were still vivid, and some would tremble at loud noises. However, the profound grief over what they had lost—family members, possessions, or friends—blunted other emotions and made many apathetic and passive. Victims of the nuclear attacks, they appeared willing to be victims afterward, too.

The effect on the Charlottesville and Albemarle residents was less pronounced. They were disoriented. For each lucky one who had a specific job to do, there were many more who were in effect unemployed. They turned inward to their families or else to friends and relatives. Their worries about the future—would there be another attack, would they go back to their old jobs, and so forth—made most days rather anxious, unproductive ones. Children particularly reflected a continuous nervousness, picked up from their elders, and had difficulty sleeping at night.

Spring changed a lot of things. A new optimism surfaced as everyone looked forward to planting, to good weather and warmth. The residents of Charlottesville had survived the first hurdle; they felt confident they could survive the next.

At the university, agronomists studied the best crops to plant in the Charlottesville area. No one was certain what effect the nuclear explosions had had on the ozone layer. If indeed the ozone was severely damaged, more ultraviolet rays could reach the crops and perhaps burn them. This effect would be more pronounced on delicate crops such as peas and beans. Instead it was suggested that potatoes and soybeans be encouraged.

The next few months in Charlottesville and Albemarle County had a slow, almost dreamlike quality. Fears of new attacks had abated. It was a time of settling into a new life-style, a severely simplified way of being, of making do. Children ate meat, cheese, or eggs rarely, adults practically never. A good pair of shoes was guarded, and worn only on special occasions.

Many people were unable to return to their former jobs. In some cases, their employers never reopened for business, their goods and services being irrelevant in the postattack society.

For some, it was relatively easy to adapt. Electronics experts set up CB and shortwave radio repair shops. Cottage industries—sandal and clothing manufacturing from recycled materials, soap and candle making—sprang up in many homes. Some workers were able to acquire new, relevant skills quickly. Others had to make do with menial jobs—burying the dead, cleaning the streets, assisting carpenters and bricklayers—that took little skill.

And then there were those who could not fit in anywhere. Many found it difficult to adapt to the idleness. Disruption of the nine-to-five work ethic was a disruption of basic psychological props, of a sense of identity. In the immediate period after the attacks, parents had concentrated on protection of their families. Once their families were no longer in immediate danger, adults were robbed of their traditional roles.

As autumn approached, a universal depression settled on the residents and refugees. Starvation had been held at bay by the planting, but crop yields were smaller than expected. No one was cold, but the weather was still fine. There seemed to be no appreciable progress toward preattack conditions.

Winter was harder than anyone had expected. Although there were few additional deaths that could be directly attributed to the nuclear blast effects or radiation, much of the surviving population was clearly weakened. Inadequate medicine, food, and shelter, plus the lingering physical and psychological effects of the attack, kept many from working effectively even when work was available. An epidemic of flu raged through the cities of the East where refugees were huddled in camps. Many died, especially children and old people.

Over a period of months, residents of Charlottesville gradually became aware of the rebuilding of rudimentary political and economic structures. The U.S. government still existed, if in a slightly reordered form.

The president, now permanently located in the Midwest along with the surviving members of Congress and the cabinet, retained the emergency powers he had taken just after the attacks.

State governments were not as well respected as before; citizens tended to blame them for the mix-ups in aid distribution.

Attempts to conscript the able-bodied to rebuild the damaged areas often failed miserably. Many simply walked off the job and returned to their families.

The nation's economy was in shambles. The bulk of the oil refining capacity had been knocked out, and only a few facilities were functioning again. The small oil wells around the country that were situated away from target areas produced more oil than the refineries could handle—and it was only a fraction of the need. Coal mining, mostly by the time-honored pick and shovel method, was the only industry that could be called booming, and there was a major migration to the mining areas by the unemployed. Agriculture, of course, was a major undertaking for much of the population. However, yields from the farms were considerably below what had been hoped for. The lack of pesticides and fertilizer cut heavily into the crops, and there was concern about a major insect invasion next summer. Food processing—wheat and corn milling particularly—showed encouraging signs of recovery.

Due to a lack of energy, raw materials, and managerial expertise, however, most industries were in disarray. The world economy was staggering from the effects of losing both the United States and the Soviet Union as suppliers and markets.

An efficient system of money still had not been reestablished. The federal government paid the military and other federal employees with dollars and tried to preserve purchasing power through a series of price controls. However, most people were reluctant to accept dollars in exchange for essentials such as food or clothing. As a result, a barter system continued to flourish and the black market, with its highly inflated prices, continued to encourage defiance of the law.

Almost a year to the day after the nuclear war between the United States and the Soviet Union, Charlottesville hosted a blue-ribbon panel of experts on reconstruction planning.

"We are in the classic race," remarked one of the participants, who had written a major study of postattack recovery some years before. "We have to be able to produce new goods and materials before we exhaust our stored supplies. We can continue to eat the wheat that is in the grain elevators of the Midwest for another year, perhaps. But after that we must have the capacity to grow new wheat. When our winter coats wear through, we must have the capacity to weave the cloth for new ones. When our railroad cars break down, we must be able to make new ones, or replacement parts. Right now we are a long way from that capacity." Privately, he and a group of conferees agreed that heavy controls on the economy, and ultimately on the population, would be the only way to get things going. Resources, both material and human, were severely limited. It was clear that if the economy did not get moving again soon, it might never.

The most basic disagreement among the participants in the conference was over the level of reconstruction that might actually be feasible. Optimists cited the phenomenal recovery of Japan and West Germany after World War II and insisted that these be the models for the United States in the next five to ten years.

Pessimists, noting the major differences between the post–World War II era and the situation of Japan and Germany, felt these examples were irrelevant or, worse, misleading.

The pessimists were divided. Some saw the nation building itself along the lines of some of the Asian nations, which boasted a small technologically advanced segment in the midst of a large agrarian or unskilled worker population, on the model of India or Indonesia. Some thought technology itself would eventually disappear from American society. "If you don't have computers to run, you don't train computer programmers," one expert was overheard to say. "After a while, in a few generations, no one remembers how the machines worked at all. They remember the important things: how to plant crops, how to train draft horses and oxen, how to make a simple pump. We will have survived biologically, but our way of life is going to be unrecognizable. In several generations, the United States is going to resemble a late-medieval society."

Because the conferees could not agree on what was a reasonable goal, much less how to get there, the conference report straddled all fences and concluded nothing. Follow-up task forces were appointed and the conferees agreed to meet again in the summer. Perhaps by then they would have a better idea of whether or not they were winning the race.

PART IV

Defusing the Bomb

11

Blankets and Big Sticks: Alternative Approaches to Security

The desire for personal security is familiar to us all. From security blankets to Social Security, it is the major preoccupation of our lives. It has always been that way for individuals, and it is the same for nations.

Early in history, men discovered they were safer in groups—from nature, from wild animals, and from one another. The size of these groups expanded from single families to groups of families (called clans) to tribes, and eventually to nations and alliances, each grouping offering more security than its constituent parts.

If we survive the next few hundred years and do find someone else out there in space, the next level of progression in security groups will presumably be planets or even whole solar systems.

The object of this book is to help us get through the next few decades without being destroyed, not by an invasion from another planet, but by a threat of our own making: nuclear weapons. The object of this chapter is to step back from the nuclear weapons issue and to take a broader look at the problem of responding to threats to security--be they threats to individuals or to nations.

Security Options

Teddy Roosevelt's prescription for national security was "Speak softly and carry a big stick." His analogy between personal and national security is important. It reminds us that nations are, and always have been, run by human beings. The problem of making our nation safe is the same now as it was in Roosevelt's time and has been throughout the two-hundred-plus years of the republic. The dangers are of the same type, and the solutions are the same, too. In fact, both—the dangers and the solutions—are the same ones we find in an ordinary schoolyard, where the little kids are threatened by the big kids. Weapons may change, but human nature remains the same. A biblical passage, a Greek tragedy, and a Shakespearean play can have as much meaning today as when they first appeared. And it should not be surprising that the basic ways of dealing with threats to security are no different today than at any other time in history.

If one group of people (family, tribe, or nation) is threatened by another group of people, there are four basic ways the former can defend its rights and independence:

By conquest: Defeat the enemy in war.

By intimidation: Arm so heavily that the enemy cannot see any gain or advantage in an attack.

By fortification: Build an impregnable barrier between you and the enemy.

By friendship: Persuade the enemy that you would both be better off if your competition were friendly and that you might even cooperate in facing other threatening parties.

Some historical perspectives on each of these options are provided below.

Conquest

Human history is filled with war—the simplest way of dealing with an enemy, but also the most dangerous, because there is no way to guarantee victory beforehand. Sometimes the conquered enemies were wiped out. More often they were assimilated. Assimilation, of course, leads to short-term management problems, but most of the time these problems go away as the people of the conquered party are absorbed into the society of the conqueror.

Most recent examples of conquest have not led to an attempt to assimilate the conquered party. For example, when Nazi Germany and Japan threatened the security of most of the other nations of the world, the response of these and other nations was to fight. In time, World War II ended with conquest of both Germany and Japan. The final terms were unconditional surrender. In neither case, however, was the conquered party assimilated. Instead, both were stripped of their military capability but permitted to retain their independence. Germany was further weakened by dividing it into two parts.

Today, both Germany and Japan have modest military forces designed for defense rather than offense. Needless to say, we would take a dim view of (and probably prevent) any attempt by either West Germany or Japan to build nuclear weapons. The Soviets would probably react even more strongly to the idea of nuclear weapons in the hands of either West Germany or East Germany—to say nothing of their horror at the prospect of a reunited Germany armed with nuclear weapons. The "never again" attitude which still persists toward Germany and Japan is one of the conqueror's rights, and it helps to explain the historical frequency of conquest as a means of guaranteeing security.

Intimidation

Deterrence of attack through intimidation—by instilling fear of the consequences—is one of the oldest and best approaches to ensuring security. When the earliest cavemen built fires at the entrances to their caves to frighten away wild animals, they were practicing deterrence through intimidation. This approach can best be characterized in schoolyard terminology as "You try that and you'll be sorry." The ancient Romans put it another way: If you want peace, prepare for war.

For this approach to be effective, it is necessary both to know what level of potential punishment will deter the enemy from attack and to be certain you can actually inflict that level of punishment. Our current approach to deterring nuclear war is basically an intimidation strategy. We have designed and protected our missile and bomber systems to ensure that we will always be able to inflict "unacceptable damage" on Russia, even if it should attack first. Chapter 12 will describe and discuss this strategy in detail.

Fortification

Under the fortification approach, one simply builds some type of impenetrable barrier around one's society. Within reasonable limits, business inside this barrier is conducted with minimal regard to what is happening outside. Medieval fortresses, surrounded by walls and moats, are an example of this approach. So is Hadrian's Wall, built by the Romans along the border between England and Scotland. The most dramatic example, of course, is the Great Wall of China—1,100 miles long, built to keep out Mongol raiders.

For most of the two hundred years that the United

States has been in existence, we have enjoyed a modified "Fortress America" status. Bordered by much weaker nations to the north and south, and by vast oceans patrolled by a strong navy, the United States has been virtually impregnable to attack. As explained in Chapter 5, all of this changed with the advent of Soviet intercontinental bombers in the mid-1950s. Even then, most citizens probably believed that our multibillion-dollar air defenses would be successful in shooting down most Soviet bombers well outside U.S. borders. Military assessments were less optimistic: the Russians had too many planes, we could never hope to shoot them all down, and the consequences of even a few nuclear weapons successfully delivered on American cities would be catastrophic. Then Soviet intercontinental bombers were followed by Soviet ICBMs. Hope for some kind of antiballistic missile system did not last long. It was great while it lasted, but the "Fortress America" concept is clearly a thing of the past.

But what about the future—the far future? There is continued speculation that technology might someday again make the "Fortress America" concept viable. The most frequently expressed hope is that *Star Wars*-type satellite-based laser or particle beam weapons, lifted into orbit by the space shuttle, could provide an impregnable shield for America. It is significant, however, that hopes for the development of such weapons are most frequently voiced by politicians and science-fiction writers, rather than scientists and engineers. This technology is in its infancy (see Chapter 15), and it is impossible to predict whether effective satellite-based systems will ever be developed—and we certainly should not count on it.

Friendship

The "making friends" approach to security is as common in human history as those of conquest, intimidation, and fortification. Sometimes societies or nations are friends from the moment they meet—as was the case (for a time) with the Pilgrims and the Indians in Massachusetts, or with the United States and France, which have remained friends since the Revolutionary War. More often, however, friendship follows enmity. The French and Germans are friends now, but only after three bitter wars in a seventy-five-year period. The French and the British were enemies until 1815 but have been friends since. We ourselves fought two wars with Britain before becoming friends. At the present time, both France and Britain have nuclear forces sufficient to destroy the top twenty cities in the United States, and kill nearly fifty million Americans. However, we do not lose one wink of sleep over this possibility. It is inconceivable that this would happen, because Britain and France are friends of the United States. The same goes for the relationship between France and Great Britain. Each has a sufficient nuclear capability to destroy the other as a functioning society. Neither weighs this prospect in its nuclear planning, because they are now friends and will be so for the foreseeable future.

The "friendship" approach is also manifest in the U.S. effort to improve relations with China. The profound change in the character of this relationship is readily apparent when one recalls the terms with which we referred to each other as recently as fifteen years ago. We were "imperialist running dogs," and they were the "yellow peril." Isn't it funny how times—and people—change?

12

You Try That and You'll Be Sorry: Deterrence through Intimidation

Since the dawn of the nuclear age, the United States has followed one basic strategy to protect itself from attack—a promise of devastating retaliation with nuclear weapons. As described in Chapter 11, we call this method of protecting our security deterring attack through intimidation, or simply deterrence.

As a practical matter, there is only one other country strong enough to attack the United States with any chance of success—the Soviet Union. The Soviet Union has threatened us verbally on innumerable occasions; for example, many of us remember former Soviet Premier Khrushchev's claim, "We will bury you." The Soviets also threatened us by placing their missiles in Cuba. But so far they have never come close to attacking the United States. Whether this will continue to be the case is, of course, open to question. Can we continue to intimidate the Russians with the threat of inflicting an unacceptable level of pain and suffering on their people and homeland? This question is the focus of this chapter.

The History of Intimidation: An Expressed Willingness to Use Nuclear Weapons

In the late 1940s it was widely believed that the Russians planned to invade Europe. Unwilling to match the Russians man for man and tank for tank, the

United States announced that, if need be, it would defend its European allies with nuclear weapons. This threat included a refusal to promise publicly that we would not use nuclear weapons or would not be the first to use such weapons.*

Deterring Soviet nuclear attack on the United States and its allies was not a problem until 1950 or so, when the Soviet Union developed its first deliverable nuclear weapons and bombers that could deliver those weapons on the United States in a one-way suicide run—suicide because the planes did not have the range to return to the Soviet Union and because the U.S. had so many more weapons and bombers that it could have easily destroyed much of the Soviet Union in a retaliatory strike. In 1954 the Soviets acquired intercontinental bombers that could reach the United States and return, but they had only a few nuclear bombs that could be delivered. By contrast, we had thousands. This massive arsenal was the cornerstone of the American policy for deterring Soviet attack known as massive retaliation.

This policy was first announced in 1954 when Secretary of State John Foster Dulles declared that any Soviet nuclear attack on the United States or its allies would be followed by an overwhelming retaliatory

---

*The commitment not to be the first to use nuclear weapons in a conflict—commonly called no first use—remains absent from U.S. and NATO policy for good reason. We still do not have the necessary conventional forces to stop a massive Soviet conventional attack on Western Europe. This would require much higher defense expenditures for all NATO nations and many more men under arms. If such an attack occurs, we most likely would have to use tactical nuclear weapons to halt the Soviet advance. This highlights one of the attractive but not well-known features of nuclear weapons—relative cheapness, or, as is often said, "more bang for the buck."

attack—an all-out attempt to destroy the Soviet Union with every means at our disposal. We begged the question "How much is enough?" We simply said that we would hit them with everything we had, and we had plenty.

Massive retaliation protected us and our allies and was cheaper than trying to match the Russians man for man and tank for tank. Within a few years, however, Soviet capability to deliver nuclear weapons on the United States had grown to such a level that the damage which the two sides could do to each other's societies was nearly the same, even though we had many more nuclear weapons than they did. As a result, a new deterrent policy called mutual assured destruction emerged.

Mutual assured destruction (or MAD, as it's sometimes called) is a policy which assumes that both sides have invulnerable or "survivable" weapons with which they could retaliate after an attack. We could destroy Soviet society, and they could destroy ours, but neither one of us could destroy *all* the other's missiles and bombers. Thus we were "assured" of destruction in response. An attack by either would literally be suicide.

Since the time of its inception, MAD has never been a particularly attractive policy. Officials accepted it pretty much in the same spirit Winston Churchill accepted democracy—the worst system of government, he said, except for all the others. Nevertheless, in spite of much complaining, MAD has remained our basic policy for deterring war since the 1960s.

The Strategic Triad

In implementing MAD, the United States has utilized nuclear forces of three different types: land-based intercontinental ballistic missiles (ICBMs), submarines armed with submarine-launched ballistic missiles (SLBMs), and manned bombers. This is the so-called strategic triad.*

Before 1960 we had only one type of strategic force—bombers. Why do we need three now? Two answers to this question are usually put forth, one historical and one theoretical. The historical explanation focuses on the interservice rivalry in the Pentagon, mainly between the air force and the navy. In the late 1940s and 1950s, the air force and the navy fought bitterly over who would get the "strategic [deterrence] mission." The army tried to get into the act, too, but was outmaneuvered and soon dropped out. Eventually a kind of peace between the services was patched together by giving a strategic mission to *both* the air force and the navy. The air force, with both ICBMs and manned bombers, got the lion's share.

The theoretical argument for the triad comes down to this: when one leg is threatened by the Soviet advances in technology, the others are still there to protect us while we try to find a solution to the threat. In the case of the Soviet threat to our high-flying B-52 bombers which emerged in the late 1950s, we found a solution—flying low. In the case of the threat to silo-based ICBMs, we have obviously not yet found a good solution, and we are glad we have two triad legs which are not currently threatened.

In the future, we may be reduced from a triad to a dyad—two legs—or we may find some new third leg, such as putting ballistic missiles on airplanes. The maintenance of an assured destruction capability is viewed as so important that most believe we should hedge not just once against breakthroughs with a dyad, but twice with a triad. In sum, to be safe, military experts believe it is imperative that we retain an

---

Triad means that our strategic forces are divided into three parts.

assured destruction capability. This means that we want to be assured that at least one leg of our triad—ICBMs, submarine missiles, or bombers—is secure against gradual improvements in Soviet weaponry or sudden technical breakthroughs which might threaten it. At least one must be able to survive a Soviet attack and penetrate to destroy Soviet cities and military targets.

The Concept of Limited War

As noted at the beginning of this chapter, it has been clear since the North Koreans attacked South Korea in 1950 that a large inventory of nuclear weapons cannot always deter conventional warfare. Nevertheless, the danger is always present that a conventional war may lead to the use of tactical nuclear weapons, something the United States considered during both the Korean and Vietnam wars. These suggestions were turned down for two reasons: fear of world public opinion, and fear that the result might be escalation to all-out nuclear war.

Like strategic nuclear weapons, tactical nuclear weapons are used to deter war. American military forces are armed with large numbers of tactical nuclear weapons which would enable us to make a limited nuclear weapon response should a conventional war turn decidedly against us. These tactical nuclear weapons are in Europe and the Far East, on land and on aircraft carriers and other ships. At the moment there are about six thousand tactical nuclear weapons in Europe, and hundreds of nuclear weapons on U.S. naval vessels. The purpose of all of these tactical nuclear weapons is to keep a nuclear war "limited" through a policy called flexible response. As implied in the term *flexible,* the hope is that the prudent use of such weapons would save U.S. forces from conventional defeat, while at the same time preventing a limited nuclear war from escalating to an all-out nuclear war involving strategic nuclear weapons.

During the early 1970s, some U.S. defense analysts began to worry that the Soviet Union might feel it could use strategic nuclear weapons in a "limited" way, possibly for a surprise attack on our land-based ICBMs and other vulnerable sites, such as airfields and submarine bases. These analysts argued that we had to be ready to respond in kind, with "limited" attacks of our own on similar Soviet targets. Previously, U.S. plans for strategic war called for the use of a minimum of hundreds of strategic weapons if we decided to use any at all. That meant either no war or a very big war. As a result, military planners began to prepare for an alternative—a kind of "tit for tat" bombing. If they hit us with a few, we would hit them with a few, and so forth.

This approach to deterrence of small nuclear attacks can be characterized as "You've got to be able to fight a nuclear war at all levels, small and large, in order to prevent it from happening at all." This policy, which is sometimes referred to as a war-fighting doctrine, has been criticized on the ground that it could make a limited nuclear war more likely—and the inability to control escalation could easily lead to all-out nuclear war. Obviously, it is difficult to know which view is correct.

The biggest challenge to the deterrence policy described above has been the emerging Soviet capability to destroy U.S. ICBM silos.* Although the U.S. mili-

---

*At present, the Soviets could destroy about 60–70 percent of U.S. ICBMs, with the number rising to 80–90 percent in a few years. We can currently destroy about 40 percent of Soviet ICBMs, with the number rising to 80–90 percent if we deploy two hundred M-X ICBMs or two hundred Trident II SLBMs.

tary for many years urged that we do the same thing, it is unlikely that we would have done so had the Soviets not taken the first step in this direction. This Soviet development made clear that they were not committed to the "live and let live" approach of not threatening the other side's "assured destruction" capability. The challenge we thus face is to find a new approach—either on our own or in cooperation with the Soviets—which will give both of us confidence in our ability to deter attack. Unless both of us feel safe, neither of us can feel safe.

Advocates of the M-X and Trident II missiles argue that these accurate new weapons, which threaten the Soviets' ICBM silos in the same manner that they threaten ours, are necessary to our getting Soviet cooperation in creating a more stable security framework. Others argue that this approach is too dangerous. In a crisis situation where both sides have the capability to destroy missile silos on the other side (sometimes called countersilo capability or counterforce capability), there would be a tremendous incentive for one side to attack the other side's ICBMs before its own ICBM silos were attacked. This is sometimes called the "use it or lose it" syndrome.

Would the Soviet Union really consider a limited attack on the U.S. ICBM force? Such an attack would obviously be extremely dangerous. Depending on wind direction and other factors, it might kill as many as twenty million Americans or as "few" as two million. An American president, knowing that retaliation would mean all-out war, *might* choose to do nothing. Or he might used manned bombers and submarine-based SLBMs to attack all remaining Soviet strategic weapons, or to attack enough Soviet cities to equalize the fatalities on both sides. If you were the American president, and knew that millions of Americans were already dead or dying, what would you do? If you were the leader of the Soviet Union, would you be confident you could get away with such a "limited" attack on U.S. stragetic forces alone?

Growing Public Concern about the Effectiveness of Intimidation

It is clear that the ability of the United States to inflict pain on an enemy has grown steadily in the nearly four decades since 1945. It continues to grow today as we deploy more and "better" nuclear weapons. Yet it is an unquestioned fact that public concern about the danger of nuclear war is higher today than in almost any period since 1945. In a September 1981 *Newsweek*/Gallup poll, for example, 65 percent of the respondents indicated that they were concerned about the possibility of nuclear war. In December 1981, an Associated Press/NBC poll found that three out of four Americans thought that the U.S. would become involved in a war of some kind in the next few years.

On the cover of this book we posed this concern as "Why do you feel scared with 10,000 nuclear weapons protecting you?"

The answer to this question lies, at least in part, in the apparent uncertainty among national security experts and the American people as a whole about the effectiveness of intimidation. To put it another way, if intimidation works, why does the answer to the question "What does it take to deter the Russians?" constantly change? If a few hundred nuclear weapons were judged adequate to deter Soviet attack thirty years ago, why are thousands needed today?

Another set of questions, even more disturbing to many people, relates to what happens when deterrence "fails." Could a crisis reach such desperate proportions that one side might launch a "preemptive first strike" against the other? Then the nuclear weapons of deterrence become the nuclear weapons of war, a frightening prospect.

Deterring Nuclear War in the Future: What Will It Take?

One way to look at the question of what it will take to deter nuclear war now and in the future is to reverse the question and ask: What would it take to make us—or the Russians—willing to go to war with nuclear weapons? If the Russians invaded Poland, would we launch nuclear weapons against the Soviet Union? Would we give up El Salvador? Berlin? Persian Gulf oil? For whom and for what are we willing to risk our own survival?

To make this question more real, put yourself in the place of the president who will have to make such decisions. Try to fill in the blanks in the left column below with something the Russians might do against which you would use nuclear weapons, knowing you would almost certainly have to pay the price listed in the right column.

Russian action you would stop	Price you would pay to stop it
1. _____	1. Destruction of one major U.S. city and its inhabitants.
2. _____	2. Destruction of twenty major U.S. cities and their inhabitants.
3. _____	3. Destruction of the thousand largest U.S. cities and destruction of all our military forces.
4. _____	4. The complete breakdown of our American social, political, and economic systems—we become an essentially preindustrial agricultural society.

You may be able to think of something that would make you, as president of the United States, willing to accept the first level of destruction in the right column. But what about the higher levels? In your thinking, you might want to keep in mind that many military experts believe your use of nuclear weapons would lead a nuclear war to escalate from the first level of destruction to the next higher level, and then the next, and then the next . . .

This exercise shows both the strength and the weakness of deterrence. The strength is that it makes both sides *very* cautious about challenging each other. The weakness is that if deterrence fails, the result could very well be catastrophic.

But what about the Soviets? How much retaliatory capability is really necessary to deter Soviet attack? Where between the "ouch" of a poke in the eye and the effective destruction of Soviet society is the level of threat which ensures that the Soviets would not launch an attack in the first place? In short, how much is "enough"? The death of twenty million Soviet people in World War II (a war they didn't start) is often cited as a measure of the loss the Soviet Union is willing to accept in warfare. Is this a good standard?

At the present time, if the Soviet Union launched a full-scale first-strike attack on the United States, enough U.S. bombers and missiles would survive to damage Russia at least to level 3. Is this retaliatory capability enough to deter a Soviet leader from launching an attack on the United States?

Deterrence and the Human Factor

So why the concern about nuclear war? Are Soviet decision makers crazy? No one who deals with them thinks so. But they are both angry *with* us and frightened *by* us—and we feel the same way toward them. Much of the concern about nuclear war lies in the risk of nonrational reaction by one side or the other. We all know from our own experience that anger and fear can lead to actions one regrets, things that seem "crazy" when we look back on them. The same is true for nations.

The reality that perfectly rational human beings sometimes do irrational things is the major weakness of deterrence through intimidation. Another weakness is the danger that things may slip out of control in a crisis, that rational acts in the short run become irrational in the long run. We call this phenomenon escalation—one thing leads to another, each step just a *little* more dangerous than the one before, until one side is fatally tempted to bluff with a nuclear weapon or use just one or two as a demonstration of will.

In an environment where deterrence of nuclear war is based on intimidation, the challenge to leaders on both sides is to think hard about their nation's vital interests, to be strong and confident without being threatening, and to avoid entanglement in confrontations from which it is difficult to extricate oneself without suffering a stinging political defeat or using nuclear weapons.

As you may have noticed, the basic question of deterrence—"How much deterrence is enough?"— remains unanswered. That reflects reality; we simply do not know the level of potential pain that is necessary to deter a Soviet nuclear attack. All we know is that to date the Soviets have not attacked us with nuclear weapons.

13

I'm O.K., You're O.K.
Negotiating Limits on Nuclear Arms

Warfare is as old as the history of man, but attempts to control the arms with which warfare is waged are relatively new. Chapter 11 described four basic ways a nation can ensure its security: through conquest, intimidation, fortification, and friendship. Arms control serves as a kind of bridge between the intimidation or fortification approaches and the approach that is most desirable—friendship, or, more precisely, friendly rivalry. It offers a way of simultaneously reducing the fear and anger and building trust.

You Don't Make Arms Control Agreements with Your Friends

One of the most challenging aspects of arms control is capsulized in the title of this section. When two (or more) parties sit down to negotiate an arms control agreement, their prior and prevailing relationship is almost certainly one of hostility. To get such parties to the negotiating table is itself an accomplishment. To achieve concrete results is even more extraordinary. As a consequence, history is paved with well-intentioned arms control negotiations that have failed. But there have been some successes.

One notable example of negotiated arms control was the agreement between the United States and England early in the nineteenth century to demilitarize the Great Lakes and the rest of the U.S.-Canadian border—the Rush-Bagot Pact. It survives to this day.

In the late nineteenth century and the early twentieth, substantial effort was devoted to various types of arms control, especially in Europe. There appear to have been two reasons for this interest. The first was the fear of a major war in Europe—a concern that existed long before World War I actually broke out. The second was the political establishment's concern that the growing socialist movement would capture the "peace" issue, a major focus of its activity. Thus government leaders sought both to quiet fears of war and to erect a political bulwark against the socialists by negotiating arms control agreements.

Of the several agreements which were signed during this period, the most important established limits for the navies of Britain, Germany, the United States, and Japan. The agreement saved a lot of money for the governments involved by rescuing them from a futile shipbuilding race. But neither this agreement nor any of the others was able to prevent World War I.

The carnage of World War I, in which millions died in trench warfare, gave birth to a new peace movement much larger than anything that had preceded it. World War I was to be "the war to end all wars," and governments sincerely hoped that instruments of international cooperation, especially the League of Nations, might prevent a new war, or at least limit the violence if one occurred. Efforts to negotiate arms limitations again took place, mainly in Geneva, but the results were similar to the pre–World War I experience: the agreements took a long time to negotiate, were only marginally effective, and did nothing to stop Hitler and the coming of World War II. Success was achieved on only one narrow issue—the use of poison gas. An agreement prohibiting the use of poison gas was signed in Geneva in 1925, and despite the fact Germany and the Allies both had large stocks of chemical agents throughout World War II, gas was never used.

Making Love to a Porcupine: A History of the U.S.-Soviet Arms Control Efforts

With the dawn of the nuclear age, there was renewed interest in negotiated limitations on the weapons of war. The continuing challenge of that effort gives vivid testimony to the problems encountered when the guy across the table is "no friend of mine."

The first attempt to limit or control nuclear arms during the postwar period came in 1946, when Bernard Baruch took a U.S. plan to the United Nations. "We are here to make a choice between the quick and the dead," Baruch said. "Let us not deceive ourselves: we must elect world peace or world destruction." The words were eloquent, but the plan would have left nuclear weapons in American hands alone, and the Russians—determined to build their own bomb—rejected it. By 1948 the wartime alliance between the Soviet Union and the West had completely collapsed. In Churchill's words, an "Iron Curtain" had fallen across Europe. We blame the Russians for this turn of events; they blame us. Regardless, the cold war was upon us.

Whatever the cause of the cold war, the result was a decade of propaganda and frantic weapons building. It was ten years before the United States and the Soviet Union again spoke civilly to each other, and it took a common threat to bring them together—the testing of nuclear weapons.

The Limited Test Ban Treaty

On March 1, 1954, the United States tested a 15-megaton hydrogen bomb—the largest the United

States has ever fired—as part of a program to develop warheads for the new Atlas missile. Unexpected winds spread a plume of radioactive fallout from the test site on Bikini atoll in the Marshall Islands over a 20,000-square-kilometer area of the South Pacific. Within this area were several inhabited islands and—at the time of the explosion—the Japanese fishing vessel *Lucky Dragon,* whose crew all suffered radiation sickness. Eventually one of them died—very much in the public eye.

By the late 1950s it had become clear that radioactive fallout from nuclear weapons testing in the atmosphere was potentially a severe health hazard. Several hundred nuclear weapons had been tested, and scientists had begun to find disturbing increases in worldwide radioactivity levels, including the level of radioactive strontium 90 in mothers' milk and children's teeth. As a step toward quieting public concern, the United States, the Soviet Union, and Great Britain agreed in 1958 to a moratorium on weapons testing in the atmosphere. This was not a formal agreement in the legal sense, but simply a promise by the three nations to stop testing nuclear weapons aboveground for an indefinite period. The Soviets broke the moratorium in late 1961—our first lesson in the fragility of nonbinding agreements.

By 1963 international concern over the health hazards of radioactive elements in the atmosphere had become so acute that a formal agreement banning such tests, the Limited Test Ban Treaty, was signed and ratified by the United States, the Soviet Union, and Great Britain. Since then all three countries have conducted nuclear tests only underground.

The Limited Test Ban Treaty (LTBT), which is still in force, was significant as the first arms control agreement of the nuclear age. It was also significant in that public concern and pressure had played a role in bringing two nations who had gone to the brink of war during the Cuban missile crisis just one year earlier to an agreement.*

The LTBT did not, of course, slow down the strategic arms race. But it did reestablish communications between the two countries and prove that international agreement on nuclear-war-related issues was possible.

Spurred by the Cuban missile crisis and the success of the LTBT, public opinion, in this country and elsewhere, supported an attempt to negotiate broader nuclear arms control measures. In the mid-1960s Secretary of Defense Robert McNamara and systems analysts in the Pentagon made the first hard case for "strategic arms control"—limits on the numbers and characteristics of strategic missiles, bombers, and defense systems. Their argument was simple: we could not make ourselves safer by adding to the destructive potential of weapons already deployed or in production. McNamara's analysts also argued that the deployment of antiballistic missiles (ABM) systems by both sides would (1) vastly complicate each side's calculations of deterrence while (2) offering no certainty of saving the United States from destruction in a nuclear war.

McNamara first persuaded President Johnson that arms control was in the American interest and then made a similar case to the Russians at a meeting with Soviet Premier Alexei Kosygin in Glassboro, New Jersey, in 1967. After thinking it over, the Russians agreed. This was the birth of the Strategic Arms Limitation Treaty (SALT) concept.

The Johnson administration plans for SALT talks with the Soviet Union were abandoned when the Soviet Union invaded Czechoslovakia in August 1968. The SALT idea was revived early in the Nixon admin-

---

*France has not signed the treaty but no longer conducts tests in the atmosphere. China has not signed, either, and continues to conduct one or two tests per year in the atmosphere.

istration, however, and again the national security arguments were persuasive. SALT also fit comfortably into the Nixon-Kissinger idea of "détente," which sought to blunt Soviet expansionism and make the Soviet Union a more constructive partner in the community of nations by building a complex arrangement of relationships between East and West. Agreements to limit arms were only one aspect of the new relationship Nixon and Kissinger hoped to achieve.

From the formal beginning of SALT in late 1969, it was clear that the process of negotiating comprehensive limitations on strategic weapons would not be easy. The United States and the Soviet Union had been mutually suspicious rivals for a generation, and both sides were deeply committed to nuclear arms as their first line of national defense. They had not discussed military matters with each other since the end of World War II. Thus the military and foreign policy analysts who saw SALT as a vehicle for enhancing American national security (and a useful element of détente) had to wage a battle on two fronts: (1) against a Soviet military proud of its weaponry and eager to build more, and (2) against elements of American society, especially in the military, cynical about Soviet intentions. Ultimately those with reservations on both sides were convinced that SALT could improve security, and in May of 1972 the first SALT agreements were signed. These included (1) a comprehensive ABM Treaty which limited both sides to low levels of antiballistic missile systems, thus avoiding an ABM race, and (2) an Interim Agreement which started, but at a minimal level, the process of controlling the numbers and characteristics of strategic offensive weapons. Both agreements were approved by the United States Senate by votes of 88–2, and it appeared that the age of nuclear arms control had truly begun.

Buoyed by popular and congressional support for SALT I and confident that no one still believed arms control was the last refuge of softheaded doves, American SALT negotiators made plans to forge a long-term agreement on limiting offensive weapons. They hoped that arms control might finally turn the world back from the nuclear abyss, but their optimism was premature.

The efforts to draft a SALT II treaty satisfactory to both sides ran into a variety of problems, including (1) the difficulty of distinguishing strategic from tactical weapons; (2) failure to agree on permissible weapons capabilities; and (3) inability to establish procedures for verifying that both parties were sticking to the agreement. It took seven years and three administrations, but all of these problems were eventually overcome, and in June of 1979 Jimmy Carter and Leonid Brezhnev met in Vienna to sign the SALT II Treaty. Only ratification by the United States Senate was required for the treaty to go into effect. Despite rumblings of opposition, the Carter administration was confident this could be achieved.

But opponents of the treaty had been hard at work. Suspicion of the Russians had revived, and some military and defense analysts argued that the treaty favored the Soviets and gave them an advantage. When the Senate SALT hearings opened in late June 1979, many senators were highly skeptical. Their concerns focused on several problem areas. Should the treaty have placed more restrictive limitations on the Soviet Backfire bomber? Was it important that the Soviets had an exclusive right to heavy missiles, bigger than the M-X? Could compliance be adequately verified? These and other questions were raised by an impressive array of former national security officials who damned the treaty either outright or with faint praise. Nevertheless, a determined group of treaty backers in the Senate and the administration kept up their efforts to secure its approval. The Joint Chiefs of Staff endorsed the treaty as "modest but useful," and finally even its harshest critics conceded that ratification seemed a certainty.

But in August and September of 1979 Senate and public support for the treaty abruptly faded in the midst of a squabble over the presence of Soviet combat troops in Cuba. The continuing troubles encountered by the treaty made it clear that the national commitment to SALT and to arms control generally was a thin veneer of hope covering a far deeper suspicion of Soviet actions and intentions. The Russian invasion of Afghanistan in December 1979 was the kiss of death. Recognizing that the last hope of ratification in his administration was gone, in January of 1980 President Carter requested that the Senate withdraw the treaty from formal consideration.

Curiously, while the SALT II Treaty remains unratified, both sides are continuing to abide by its terms. Relations between the two superpowers have not been worse since the Cuban missile crisis, yet neither has chosen to take on the responsibility—and the political burden—of delivering a final blow to the treaty. On the U.S. side, the treaty itself remains in the hands of the Senate, gathering dust in some obscure file drawer, where it is likely to stay.

As this book goes to press, new negotiations on strategic arms limitations are anticipated to begin in the late spring of 1982. Two possible approaches might be taken in those negotiations. The first would be to "fix" the SALT II Treaty with modest changes that would make it more acceptable to the Reagan administration. With goodwill on *both* sides, such a revised SALT II Treaty might be completed in six to eighteen months. The second approach would be to try to negotiate a new treaty with deep reductions (say, 25 to 50 percent) in strategic force levels, more comprehensive qualitative limits, and more intrusive monitoring or verification measures. Such negotiations would take from three to five years and possibly even longer.

Arms Control to Date—What Have We Learned

The history of arms control up to now has been a tale of great hope and modest accomplishment—the characteristics of any venture into new and unfamiliar ground. The modest accomplishments include two countries armed to wage nuclear war against each other sitting down to explore means by which the risk and consequences of such a war could be reduced. That such discussions took place at all demonstrates both sides' awareness of the dangers inherent in unchecked nuclear weapons rivalry.

Whether we can ultimately bridge the chasm between the intimidation and fortification approaches to security and the friendship approach is not really a challenge to arms control per se. Rather, it is a challenge to our willingness to strive for that level of social and cultural development at which differences can be settled by negotiation and other peaceful means, rather than by conflict.

This challenge is not just a challenge to nations but to national leaders and the people in whose interest they act. We all know how difficult it is to "rise above ourselves." In some cases we can only do this when threatened by factors outside our control. Could the awesome threat of a nuclear holocaust serve as such an outside factor? Will this threat enable people and nations to make the kind of leap to a higher level of development which, like the abolition of slavery and the advent of universal education, has most marked the truest progress of human civilization?

14

Know the Opposition: A Scouting Report on the Russians

One of the oldest admonitions in any competition is "Know the opposition." Athletic teams in every sport devote considerable time and energy to scouting reports, old game films, analysis of opposition strengths and weaknesses, and related activities leading up to a head-to-head clash. This same approach is used in the competition of international relations.

As we anticipate a possible head-to-head clash with the Soviet Union we are led to an extensive scouting and analysis of past Soviet strategies and tactics, current Soviet offensive and defensive capabilities, and future Soviet capabilities, plans, and actions. The stakes are extraordinarily high in the international competition between two superpowers such as the United States and the Soviet Union, so "knowing the opposition" is of paramount importance for both.

Knowing the Russians: No Easy Task

In the period since World War II, we have spent a lot of time and energy analyzing Soviet military strategy and tactics as they were practiced in World War II and the various armed conflicts in which the Soviet Union has been directly or indirectly involved since then. As supplemented by our scrutiny of past Soviet weapons development and production, these analyses have given us a pretty good picture of how the Soviet Union goes to war. The bulk of current U.S. effort to know the Soviet Union is directed toward obtaining straight factual information on current Soviet military capabilities. As previous chapters have described, we know a great deal about the numbers and performance characteristics and reliability of Russian bombers, missiles, submarines, and so forth. Thus, in the realm of current military capabilities, we know the opposition pretty well. However, the picture is far less clear when we turn our attention to future Soviet military capabilities and how these capabilities might be employed.

In the past we have done reasonably well in projecting future Soviet weapons force levels, although frequently the Soviets have reached these levels a year or two earlier or later than our best estimates. A much greater concern in the projection of future capabilities is the possibility of a major Soviet technological breakthrough which could put us at a serious disadvantage in the event of war. We put a lot of resources into espionage activities to detect any adverse developments in this area, and so far we have never been caught off guard.

When examining a possible future confrontation with the Soviet Union, it is of crucial importance that we look at Soviet goals and objectives, underlying philosophies and ideologies, and so on. This examination will lead us to ask why and in what circumstances the Soviet Union would choose to use all those weapons in their arsenal. Does the Soviet Union want to conquer the world, or just be ranked Number 1? Will they settle for a tie? Can the Soviet Union imagine a future in which we are a friendly rival, or do they see us as a deadly threat to their existence which ultimately must be destroyed? What motivates the Soviet leader? Does he want to win the Nobel Peace Prize and be a hero in his time and in the history books? Is he a plodding but sincere bureaucrat just trying to guarantee the security of his people, or is he the devil incarnate, trying to destroy the Judeo-Christian, democratic, capitalist world? The answers to these questions are crucial if we are to deal intelligently with the Soviet Union, but so far in this country we have never been able to agree on those answers.

It Started with the Czars: A Brief Overview of Russian History

The reader will note that at times in this book (and elsewhere) the terms *Russia* and *the Soviet Union* are used interchangeably. This is consistent with common parlance, where one hears expressions like "You can't trust the Russians" and "Soviet achievements in space" applied to the same country. As any student of "Russian" or "Soviet" history knows, however, this interchanging of names is technically wrong, since Russia is only one (albeit the dominant one) of the nations that make up the Union of Soviet Socialist Republics. The other nations in the Soviet Union (the Ukraine, the Baltic republics, the largely Moslem Central Asia republics, and so forth) all have individual histories and cultures—a fact that does not escape the Soviet leadership.

The history of the Soviet Union prior to the Revolution of 1918 is the history of Russia and the Russian czars whose wars and conquests dominated the region that now constitutes the world's largest nation in land area. As kings went, the czars were probably worse than most. Russia was poor and isolated, the peasants were exploited, and the monarchy and associated bureaucracy were small, highly elitist, and suspicious of foreigners. The czars themselves were unusually insecure and preoccupied with appearances. Under the monarchy Russia was able to dominate the region and defeat Napoleon in the early nineteenth century, but barely able to hold its own against the Germans in World War I. The old ruling elite was replaced by a new ruling elite whose cruel exploitation and oppression of the people was at least as bad as the czars' for a generation or more. The United States chose not to recognize this new regime until 1932, hardly an easy beginning for a bilateral relationship.*

In 1941 Germany cast aside the mutual nonaggression pact the two countries had signed two years before, and invaded the Soviet Union. World War II and the successful Allied effort to halt Nazi Germany opened a new era in U.S.-Soviet relations. The Russians were suddenly our friends—but the friendship barely survived the war. The Soviet Union, which had suffered the most severe losses of any nation in World War II (20 million dead), chose to maintain its political and military control over those Eastern European nations (and roughly a third of Germany) in its possession when the war ended—ostensibly as a buffer against future invasions. This act, which the Western powers condemned as absolutely unjustifiable, quickly led to a deterioration in relations between the Soviet Union and its World War II allies. Thus began the cold war.

A Mystery Inside an Enigma

We spend several billion dollars per year on intelligence collection systems designed to obtain factual information on Soviet military capabilities. We would gladly spend twice that to obtain information of comparable quality on "where they're coming from."

In the late 1930s Winston Churchill characterized the Soviet Union as "a riddle wrapped in a mystery inside an enigma." Now, forty years later, we know the Soviets better but are still baffled by many aspects of Soviet behavior. This is in part because the Soviet Union is a closed and highly secretive society with a

---

*The United States also sent a division of 6,000 troops to Russia in 1918 to help those Russians who were trying to halt the communist takeover.

penchant for propaganda, exaggeration, and disinformation; as a result, there are no unassailable "experts" on the Soviet Union.

As with the fabled blind men who examined different parts of an elephant and drew different conclusions about the nature of the beast, respected longtime students of the Soviet Union provide widely varying explanations for different aspects of historical Soviet behavior. And their ability to predict Soviet behavior—the ultimate test of expertise—in virtually every case has been abysmal. This observation is not a criticism of so-called Sovietologists. Rather, it is a description of the challenge of understanding and dealing with a country like the Soviet Union.

It is more difficult to explain why there are, as best we can tell, no thoroughly knowledgeable experts on the United States in the Soviet Union—in spite of the existence of an Institute of the U.S.A. and Canada. While we sometimes have trouble understanding our own behavior, Soviet actions at times suggest that they have little or no understanding of U.S. goals and policies in the international arena, much less the U.S. political system. It seems particularly difficult for them to imagine a system in which popular will, with all of its unpredictability, can play such a key role in national decision making.

Perhaps the best example of this is the apparent Soviet inability to predict the strength of the U.S. response to Soviet actions. For example, when the Soviets chose to build accurate missiles that could destroy U.S. silo-based ICBMs, they violated one of the governing taboos of the U.S.-Soviet competition *as the U.S. had defined it.*

There had been much public discussion in the U.S. on the issue of developing threats to Soviet ICBMs—a capability we could have achieved in the early to mid-1970s. However, in a much-heralded letter to then Senator Edward Brooke of Massachusetts, President Nixon rejected the idea of threatening Soviet ICBMs as destabilizing. He felt it would alarm them and gain us nothing in the end. Was the Soviet political leadership aware of this when they authorized the Soviet ICBM program which allowed them to threaten us in exactly that way? What did Soviet military leaders, who certainly understood the military significance of the move, tell them? Was the political leadership invited to weigh the possible consequences: the impact on détente, a difficult and eventually unsuccessful struggle for SALT II ratification, a U.S. commitment to an M-X program which in turn threatens Soviet ICBMs? We do not know the answer to these questions, but the incident gives vivid—and worrisome—testimony to Soviet lack of understanding of U.S. attitudes and policies, and vice versa.

We thus have a double dilemma: the world's two superpowers hold the future of civilization in their hands, and neither "knows the opposition" very well.

The Russians: Two Views

There is probably no subject in international relations on which there is more disagreement than the question "What is with the Russians?" The authors of this book claim no unique insight into this question and have thus decided to present two contrasting views held by different groups of Russian-watchers. The reader is not expected to conclude that one or the other is the proper view, but rather to glean some understanding of the problems and the uncertainties which we face in dealing with the Soviet Union and its current leadership.

In examining these two views, it should be kept in mind that the way we see the Russians determines the way we try to deal with them. Thus, the fact that responsible scholars have such divergent views on Soviet goals and motivations helps to explain some of the uncertainty and changes in U.S. policy toward the Soviet Union over the last thirty-seven years. Before presenting the two views in detail, let's examine the view of the Soviet Union that was put forth in 1947 as U.S.-Soviet relations deteriorated and the cold war began. This early postwar perspective, which had a tremendous impact on U.S. policy, was articulated by George F. Kennan, a noted Soviet scholar and later ambassador to the Soviet Union. In a now famous article in the journal *Foreign Affairs* entitled "The Sources of Soviet Conduct," Kennan attempted to explain the broad goals behind Soviet foreign policy, the effect of these goals in the postwar world, and what they might mean for American policy makers.

The Soviets, Kennan claimed, could not be our friends except under dire circumstances, because they adhered dogmatically to an ideology and a policy that saw the democratic capitalism of the United States and Western Europe as their natural enemy. In Kennan's view, the Marxist-Leninist theory to which the Soviet leadership was committed propelled them down a road whose major objective was the worldwide destruction of the private ownership of the means of production and the capitalist system.

This article and this argument provided the ideological basis for the U.S. approach to the Soviet Union for much of the cold war. Now for today's two views.

A Defense-Minded Soviet Union

Over thirty-five years later, Kennan is again at the center of a debate about the goals and motivations of the Soviet Union. His current view of the Soviets was set forth in an October 1981 *New Yorker* magazine article, "Two Views of the Soviet Problem." In that article, he argues that many students of Soviet behavior neglect the possibility that the current Soviet military stance is motivated to a large extent by defensive considerations—that the Soviets do feel encircled and threatened by the United States and its allies. He argues that the Soviet leadership has a narrow view of the best way to guarantee their own security, that they are

> . . . prisoners of many circumstances: prisoners of their own past and their country's past; prisoners of the antiquated ideology to which their extreme sense of orthodoxy binds them; prisoners of the rigid system of power that has given them their authority; but prisoners, too, of certain ingrained peculiarities of the Russian statesmanship of earlier ages.

Kennan sees the Soviet leaders as reluctant to use their powerful armed forces to expand their sphere of influence, yet easily ". . . frightened into taking actions that would seem to have this aim." He sees their desire to increase their influence in the Third World countries of Africa, Asia, and Latin America as similar in origin to our desire to have the same degree of influence there. At the same time, Kennan notes that the Soviets are potentially dangerous and display

> . . . certain disquieting tendencies, which oblige Western policymakers to exercise a sharp vigilance even as they pursue their efforts toward peace. I believe that these tendencies reflect not so much any thirst for direct aggression as an oversuspiciousness, a fear of being tricked or outsmarted, an exaggerated sense of prestige, and an interpretation of Russia's defensive needs so extreme—so extravagant and so far-reaching—that it becomes in itself a threat, to the security of other nations.

An Offense-Minded Soviet Union

On the other side of this debate is a lineup of other prestigious figures, including editor of *Commentary* magazine Norman Podhoretz, Harvard professor and member of the White House staff in the Reagan administration Richard Pipes, and the exiled Russian novelist Alexander Solzhenitsyn. These individuals tend to focus on the fundamentals of Communist doctrine as the principal explanation for Soviet behavior. In Pipes's words:

> Marxism-Leninism is by its very nature a military doctrine, the child of the age of Social Darwinism, which views history as the record of uninterrupted class warfare and which advocates the continuation of a class war as a means of abolishing for once and for all, classes and the exploitation of man by man. The end objective of Soviet global policy is a world from which private ownership of the means of production has been banished and the constituent states are, with minor variations, copies of the Soviet state.

Advocates of this school of thought see the Soviet leaders as ideologically motivated to expand their power, even when that might threaten international peace. They believe the buildup of Soviet military forces can only be explained by aggressive intentions toward other nations. They point to the subjugation of Eastern Europe, the support for the North Korean invasion of South Korea, and Soviet backing of revolutionary movements in Cuba, Angola, Ethiopia, Afghanistan, and elsewhere in the Third World.

Norman Podhoretz provided a summary assessment of this view in a 1980 *Commentary* article. He argued:

> The Soviet Union is a revolutionary state, exactly as Hitler's Germany was, in the sense that it wishes to create a new international order in which it would be the dominant power and whose character would be determined by its national wishes and its ideological dictates. In such an order, there would be no more room for any of the freedoms we now enjoy than there is at this moment within the Soviet Union, or any of the other Communist countries, even the

most lightly ruled of which are repressive beyond the most lurid nightmares of a politically pampered American experience. In short, the reason Soviet imperialism is a threat to us is not merely that the Soviet Union is a superpower bent on aggrandizing itself, but that it is a Communist state armed to the teeth, and dedicated to the destruction of the free institutions which are our heritage and our glory. In resisting the advance of Soviet power . . . we are fighting for freedom and against Communism, for democracy and against totalitarianism.

Common Areas of Agreement

Despite the contrasts in these two views of the Soviet Union, there are some areas of agreement (although each side varies in its emphasis on different points).

- The many invasions of Russia and the Soviet Union from the West have made the Soviet leadership extraordinarily sensitive to this danger.

- The destruction and loss of life which the Soviets suffered in World War II have left them with an indelible "never again" attitude. They see the possibility of another destructive war as very real—to be both avoided, if possible, *and* prepared for, if deterrence of war fails.

- The Soviets feel they are encircled by hostile powers which pose a genuine threat to their security. In fact, every other nation which acknowledges nuclear weapons capability points those weapons at the Soviet Union.

- The Soviets feel very much alone—an "us against them" attitude. They ascribe their isolation in part to their being Russians, and in part to their being at the forefront of the revolution of the proletariat or working class.

- It is significant that Russia and the Soviet Union have never known anything but autocratic regimes.

- Military power and the military itself play an unusually large role in Soviet society, at least in part because it has been the military that "saved" the nation in the past.

- What we think of as a lot of military power, they think of as a modest amount.

- Their embracing of a strongly anticapitalist ideology inevitably puts them at odds with the Western capitalist democracies.

- They see expansion as an indivisible part of an ongoing revolution.

Some specialists on the Soviet Union have further argued that the Soviet approach to national security is that everyone else should feel a little insecure. If this is indeed their objective, they have certainly succeeded.

Stepping Back: What Does This Mean for Nuclear War?

Seeing the Soviet Union as a highly security-conscious, almost paranoid nation suggests that as a first step toward reducing the risk of nuclear war we should take pains to persuade the Soviets that we do not pose a threat to their security. To a large degree, this view is the theoretical bulwark of arms control negotiations between the two countries.

Alternatively, seeing the Soviet Union as an aggressive, highly ideological, revolutionary regime bent on destruction of the United States suggests that negotiations of any kind are hopeless because, given their ideology and goals, the Soviets cannot be trusted to keep agreements.

Because of our inability to resolve these conflicting views, the U.S. has tended to pursue first one strategy and then the other, and sometimes both. For example, we only recently negotiated a SALT II Treaty with the Russians even while both countries were spending billions to upgrade the strategic nuclear weapons pointed at each other. But then detection of a Soviet combat brigade in Cuba and the invasion of Afghanistan reminded us of the expansionist, revolutionary orientation of the Soviet leadership, and we backed off from SALT II ratification. The SALT-Afghanistan experience, coupled with the Soviet role in the suppression of the Solidarity movement in Poland, calls attention to a further uncertainty in Soviet behavior—risk taking. What risks are the Soviets prepared to take to achieve modest, even marginal, "revolutionary" objectives? While their central goal, like that of all nations, is self-preservation, their secondary objective of revolutionary expansion can lead to moves which increase the risk of nuclear war. Insight to their weighing of this risk-taking dilemma is one of the most challenging issues for their adversaries.

The contrasting views of the Soviet Union presented above highlight our difficulties in deciding what the Soviets are up to and in formulating a foreign and military policy to deal with them. The basic question remains: despite our uncertainty concerning Soviet intentions, can they be brought into a constructive partnership committed to reducing the risk of nuclear war? Since Eisenhower, every American president has confronted the issue of nuclear war and has concluded that trying to engage the Soviets in such a partnership was worth the effort. Yet none has wavered in his determination to maintain a formidable strategic nuclear force pointed directly at the Soviet Union while that effort was in progress.

PART V

You Ain't Heard Nothing Yet

15

Space Invaders and *Star Wars:*
Military Technologies Now on the Drawing Boards

Star Wars! Now, there was a movie! Moon-sized space stations, star fighters, a super passing gear called hyperspace, killer laser beams, light swords. It was great entertainment, just right for the kid in all of us, a fantasy excursion to the outer limits of imaginary warfare. But it's only science fiction, right? Maybe— and maybe not.

Back in the 1940s they used to call it Buck Rogers war. A handful of visionaries saw what was coming, but the military establishment thought missiles and space ships were a joke. The word *rocket* dropped out of use. Bomber pilots were running the air force, and what they wanted was planes—big ones and fast ones.

In December 1945, the Chief of the Office of Scientific Research and Development, Vannevar Bush, told everybody to stop dreaming about rocket-delivered weapons. "In my opinion," he said, "such a thing is impossible and will be impossible for many years. The people who have been writing these things that annoy me have been talking about a 3,000-mile high angle rocket shot from one continent to another carrying an atomic bomb, and so directed as to be a precise weapon which would land on a . . . city. I say technically I don't think anybody in this world knows how to do such a thing, and I feel confident it will not be done for a very long period of time to come. I think we can leave it out of our thinking."

But the "high angle rocket"—an early term for a vertically launched ballistic missile—was no dream. Just a dozen years later, in the fall of 1957, the Soviet Union launched the first man-made satellite, called *Sputnik*, into orbit around the earth. It weighed only 400 pounds, and all it could do was broadcast electronic beeping sounds. In 1969, less than fifteen years after that, a Saturn rocket lifted an Apollo spacecraft weighing 100,000 pounds into orbit—and the whole world watched on its television sets as the spacecraft took human beings to the moon. Today, there are hundreds of satellites in orbit, and the space shuttle has proved it can put 60,000 pounds of "whatever you want" safely into space. Before long the shuttle will be doing just that on a monthly basis.

Not bad for mere earthlings. Today's realities were yesterday's science fiction. What does that mean for the future?

Space Warfare: Yesterday and Today

From the moment of *Sputnik*'s first beep it was clear that space offered tremendous potential for military applications. The first steps were communications and weather satellites, soon followed by spy satellites which took pictures of the Soviet Union from a hundred miles above the earth. Satellites also intercepted all kinds of hitherto inaccessible radio communications. Then came satellites that could detect missile launches—the first warning we would have that nuclear war had begun. But none of these were really weapons, and, unless one fell on you from space— possible, but unlikely—they couldn't hurt a flea.

But eventually, of course, real warfare came to space. The Russians were first, in the mid-1960s, with a so-called Fractional Orbital Bombardment System (FOBS) which launched a nuclear weapon into orbit and then fired retro-rockets to "deorbit" the weapon to a target in the United States. The system was very inaccurate and is no longer deployed. In 1968 the Soviets began testing a system designed to destroy satellites (called an antisatellite or ASAT system).

Since satellites are very fragile, it is very easy to disable or destroy one if you can get close to it. Thus the Soviet ASAT system was itself a satellite—a killer satellite—designed to get close enough (about a mile) to a U.S. satellite to kill it with conventional high explosives and shrapnel. The Soviets have tested this system almost twenty times, and it is probably operational, although it can only reach U.S. satellites at altitudes below about 500 miles. (The altitude of satellites varies from about 100 miles to 22,000 miles.)

The United States has also been working on killer satellite systems, but less actively. None of the early systems reached the testing stage, and a new approach is now being tried. Scheduled for testing in 1983, this new method of satellite killing involves use of an F-15 interceptor aircraft to launch a small "homing vehicle" into orbit. This "homing vehicle" would use an infrared detector or a radar to get close enough to a Soviet satellite to destroy it. Plans for a follow-on killer satellite system much like the Soviet Union's but capable of destroying satellites at higher altitudes are also being pursued.

Many analysts have urged a ban on satellite killers, in part because they threaten warning systems and thus, in a crisis, might make war more likely. In 1978 the United States and the Soviet Union began to discuss such a ban, but the negotiations were suspended after the Soviet invasion of Afghanistan in December 1979.

So much for satellites killing satellites, but what about satellites killing other things?

So far, no satellites capable of killing other objects (missiles, bombers, or targets on the ground) have been placed in orbit. But, as the next section demonstrates, there are a lot of ideas for lethal systems of this sort for the future.

Space Warfare: Tomorrow and Tomorrow and Tomorrow

The near future—say, the next two decades—will probably see the development of ever more sophisticated and effective means for destroying orbiting satellites. These could include ground-based systems such as high-powered lasers which could burn holes in satellites, ground-launched interceptors similar to current U.S. and Soviet designs, or orbiting mines which would shadow enemy satellites and then be detonated on command when the war begins. In addition, new antisatellite systems will probably be able to destroy satellites at the 22,000-mile altitude* where both sides maintain important communications, spy, and warning satellites.

As you can see, none of the systems described so far approach *Star Wars* technology, but such things are also on the drawing boards or—perhaps more precisely—on the backs of envelopes. The candidate technologies are called (1) particle beam weapons, and (2) lasers.

Particle beam weapons are basically atomic shotguns which fire atomic particles such as protons, elec-

---

*At a 22,000-mile altitude, a satellite goes around the earth every twenty-four hours, i.e., at the same rate that the earth turns. Thus, a satellite at a 22,000-mile altitude at the equator will always remain over the same spot on the earth. Such satellites are said to be in synchronous or stationary orbit with respect to the earth. Satellites of this type are used to detect missile launches from the heat given off by the rocket plumes—the billowing trail behind rockets—which can be seen by satellite infrared detection systems.

trons, or neutrons (Chapter 1), instead of the small lead pellets of the conventional shotgun. But, whereas the pellets from a shotgun spread rapidly, an effort is made to limit the spreading of a particle beam so that the beam will remain an effective weapon at distances of hundreds or even thousands of miles.

Scientists have been producing high-energy particle beams in cyclotrons and other devices for decades. But the laboratory devices require a vacuum, and even large accelerators produce only a weak beam of particles. Doesn't sound like much of a weapon prospect, does it?

Space, however, provides the best vacuum of all, and our ability to put large objects in space continues to grow. These factors, combined with steady progress in the physics and engineering of particle beam weapons, have led to increased interest in space-based particle beam weapons. The hope—we are not far enough along to call it a plan—is that someday we can place a system of dozens of particle beam weapons in orbit at an altitude of a few hundred miles and then use them to shoot down attacking bombers and missiles.

Before you breathe a sigh of relief—At last! A real antimissile system!—you should realize that we are not there yet and may never get there. The physics and engineering problems which remain to be solved are prodigious, and the most optimistic talk about these weapons comes from politicians and generals, not from scientists and engineers.

The story with laser weapons is basically the same. Lasers are like flashlights, only the beam of light is very intense, highly focused, and entirely of one wavelength.* As a result, laser devices can produce power-

---

*If you have ever dialed a radio or seen a rainbow, you understand the concept of wavelength. The different colors of the rainbow are all different wavelengths, as are the different settings on your radio dial.

ful beams that travel great distances without spreading.

The problems in the way of effective laser weapons are basically the same as those for particle beam weapons. In a nutshell, we're getting better at it, but we still can't be sure the restraining physics and engineering problems can be overcome. Current laser generators are much too heavy, the laser beam is not intense enough, and it is extremely difficult to point the laser accurately at what you're trying to kill.

If by now you've cooled on the prospect of *Star Wars* weapons saving the United States from Soviet nuclear attack in the foreseeable future, that's the right attitude to take. But maybe you're afraid instead that the Russians will get there first, as they did with *Sputnik*. Forget it. They have the same problems we do, and unless they've made a dramatic discovery—of which there is *no* evidence—they are probably about where we are.

It will be at least a decade, and maybe several, before we know for sure whether it is even possible to design a particle beam or laser system that might shoot down bombers or missiles. And then it would take another five to ten years to build an effective system— one which could simultaneously shoot down not just a few dozen objects but over a hundred bombers and as many as a thousand missiles. It will probably also have to destroy the missiles in the few minutes of the boost phase (that is, before they release their warheads), since finding and killing much smaller, faster, and tougher warheads would be very difficult. Also keep in mind that airplanes flying at low altitude would be less vulnerable than missiles, because the atmosphere scatters particle beams and bends and distorts laser beams.

In the face of problems and uncertainties of this magnitude, it is legitimate to ask whether we want to move the U.S.-Soviet military competition to space. Many people argue that we should move beyond mere antisatellite negotiations to include a ban on all space-based weapon systems. (The placing of nuclear weapons in space is already banned by the 1967 Outer-Space Treaty.) Others argue that if we have a chance to beat the Russians in this game because of our advanced technology and the space shuttle, we should give it a try—even if it takes fifty years. What would you do if you were president?

Invisible Airplanes and Other Ghosts

Another future development you have probably heard a lot about is called Stealth. This technology is designed to make airplanes and cruise missiles far less "visible" to radars and other detection systems than they are today. As you know from Chapter 4, intercontinental bombers—the "air-breathing" leg of the U.S. strategic triad—offer the particular advantage of being recallable. This is one of the main reasons that the Pentagon wants to keep manned bombers in the U.S. strategic force for as long as possible. Stealth covers a variety of schemes to make aircraft and cruise missiles more difficult to detect. In fact, some of the early news stories about the Stealth concept leave the impression that this technology could make airplanes literally invisible. Sounds great if it can be done. But can it?

Bombers (and even cruise missiles) are large, relatively slow-moving metal objects which in principle can be detected in many different ways. To date, the best detection devices have been radars, which detect aircraft and cruise missiles in the same way that the local radar trap detects your car—by bouncing radio signals off metal and sharp edges. Bombers and cruise missiles also have continuously operating jet engines that produce a lot of heat, which can be picked up by infrared sensors operating at wavelengths invisible to the naked eye. Because of their size, bombers and cruise missiles can also be seen in the normal way—by the naked eye or television cameras—as long as it is daylight. Finally, these aircraft all make noise, another potential means of detection.

Stealth technology seeks to minimize the ability of radars and infrared detectors to detect aircraft. For radars, this is called reducing the radar cross section, and for infrared sensors, reducing the infrared signature. As you might imagine, reducing the detectability of aircraft is not going to be easy. But some progress has been made. We have found that there are materials which absorb radar signals instead of bouncing them back as clearly as bare metal. We have also found that certain shapes for wings and engine inlets minimize the return signal from a radar. Other techniques have been developed to cool the exhaust of jet engines, thus reducing the infrared signature of aircraft.

It remains to be seen whether the Stealth approach to minimizing the detectability of aircraft can keep ahead of improvements in radars, infrared, and other detection systems. In particular, satellite-based radar and infrared detection systems pose a major challenge to this effort. Nevertheless, it may be possible for Stealth technology to keep one jump ahead of defense measures so that we can buy an extra ten, twenty, or maybe even thirty years of usefulness for manned bombers.

Finding Submarines: The Ultimate Needle in a Haystack

Detection of submarines on patrol is the most challenging technical problem of the nuclear competition, and one of the reasons we are so confident about the deterrent value of our ballistic missile submarine force.

At first examination, you might observe that there are many characteristics of submarines, especially nuclear submarines, that would make them detectable—and, in principle, you would be right. But in practice, the ocean is a wonderful place to hide in, and, in spite of tens of billions of dollars in expenditures, finding and destroying submarines—called antisubmarine warfare (ASW)—remains an extraordinary technical challenge, especially for the Soviet Union, whose technological development lags behind that of the United States in this and so many other areas. Consider, if you will, the following list of potential techniques that the Soviets might use for detecting American submarines.

1. *Passive acoustic:* simply listening, the decades-old method of detecting submarines. It doesn't work; U.S. submarines are just too quiet. We have far better listening devices, and we can only hear our own subs at very short ranges.

2. *Active acoustic:* the sound version of radar—you send out a signal and listen for what comes back. Works at very short distances—say, a mile or two. But it's easy to evade; the prey can hear the hunter.

3. *Magnetic anomaly detection:* trying to detect the thousands of tons of metal that make up a submarine. If you can get within a few hundred yards of a submarine, it works fine—but you've got to find the submarine before you can get that close.

4. *Radioactivity:* detection of the radiation from the nuclear reactor in a nuclear-powered sub. Sorry—there is very little of it, especially compared to the natural background, and water absorbs it very quickly.

5. *Surface disturbances:* waves on the surface which result from the submarine's "pushing" through the water a hundred feet below. An interesting idea, but it is extraordinarily difficult to detect such surface waves because of the waves already on the surface—the ocean is no glass tabletop.

6. *Lasers:* using the blue and green wavelengths of natural light—which penetrate to great depths in the ocean, as any scuba diver knows. In principle, a satellite- or aircraft-based blue-green laser might search for subs. It's an interesting idea, but the technical problems (for example, false alarms from whales) are prodigious.

The list goes on. As you can see, a lot of scientific efforts go into the search for viable submarine detection. To date, however, submarines—especially the quiet submarines built by the United States—remain undetectable. Should there be a technological breakthrough that identifies a practical means of detecting submarines, the impact would be very far-reaching—tantamount to perfection of a laser or particle beam ABM system. It may come through improvements in one of the techniques cited above, but don't bet on it. Some of the best scientists and engineers in this country run billion-dollar programs just to make sure these technologies won't work for us and the Russians.

But then, Vannevar Bush was very wrong about rockets. . . .

In the Interim

We can't count on miracles. Americans in particular seem to think science can do anything—develop a cure for cancer, find a source of energy to take the place of oil, solve the problem of radioactive waste, eliminate auto pollution.

You name the problem, and a scientist somewhere is working on a technical solution. We tend to take the same approach with military problems. The Pentagon spends hundreds of millions of dollars a year on research and development efforts to find high-technology solutions to military problems. But nuclear war is a political problem, not some glitch that can be remedied technologically. And certainly one of the lessons of the nuclear age is that new technology is very unlikely to solve the problem of nuclear war. Quite the contrary. When the *Star Wars* weapons finally arrive, it is very unlikely that they will be part of the solution—but instead just another part of the problem.

But What if It All Works?

In the sections above, the prospect of future exotic technologies achieving practical military application has been downplayed—and for good reason. But suppose the many technical barriers to these applications are overcome and today's science-fiction fantasies do become reality. And then suppose we fight a nuclear war. What would it be like? Try this scenario.

It is the year 2020, and an alliance of socialist nations in Latin America has declared war on Brazil. The U.S.-Brazilian alliance calls for U.S. aid in the event of any aggression against Brazil, and the Soviet Union appears ready to come to the support of its socialist partners. The Brazilian nuclear capability consists of ten transport aircraft converted to bombers and three dozen nuclear-armed mobile IRBMs mounted on rivercraft which achieve survivability by hiding in the dense foliage overhanging the many tributaries of the Amazon. The United States supplied the missile boosters, salvaged from retired Trident I SLBMs. The Latin American Socialist Alliance, headed by Argentina, possesses a dozen Backfire bombers and two missile-carrying submarines supplied by the Soviets.

After the first nuclear exchange between the two sides, it is clear that escalation to all-out nuclear war between the superpowers is genuinely possible. At this point the president of the United States is evacuated to Cape Canaveral and launched into orbit in the National Emergency Command Translunar Integrator

(NECTI) satellite known as Necktie. As it heads for its
first lunar circumnavigation secure communications
are established with the orbiting air force, navy, and
army military officers whose shuttle-launched space
stations contain the proton beam weapons which defend the United States—and of course themselves—
from missile attack.

Meanwhile the Soviet president and Communist
party general secretary flies to Vladivostok and boards
the deep-diving, hydrogen/oxygen-powered titanium
submarine which serves as his wartime command
post. Within minutes the submarine is at its patrol
depth of 1,000 feet and in full communication with the
Soviet General Staff through the same kind of 1,000-
mile-square low-frequency transmitter which the U.S.
military sought but was unable to build because of
domestic objections to its potential environmental impact. The Soviets even named their system Sanguine
as a thumb in the eye to the American military, which
had once used this name for their own planned system.

As the crisis grows the president instructs the U.S.
Air Force commander in the Jabberwocky satellite to
begin the radar and laser satellite scans of the Northern Pacific to search for both the Soviet missile submarines and the Soviet command submarine, referred to
by the U.S. military as Deep Throat.

As the scans begin they are detected by the Soviets,
and jamming transmitters secretly implanted in a thousand whales by the Soviets over the past ten years
produce false returns indistinguishable from real submarines. The U.S. Colossus data-processing satellite
immediately relays the signals to the U.S. Air Force
computer facility in Omaha, where an effort is made to
unscramble the signals to find the real submarines.

Suddenly a Red Rooster space booster is launched
from its mountain silo in the Urals. As the U.S. radar
and infrared satellite systems track the first and second
stages of the booster it becomes obvious that it is
heading for Necktie. But the booster suddenly disap-

pears from both the radar and infrared tracking screens. The truth of the matter is clear: the third stage and payload of the missile has Stealth technology for both radar and infrared detection. Necktie is in danger!

When the president receives word that an invisible attacker appears to be on the way, she instructs her military aide to patch her to the Soviet president through the hot line. Unknown to the Soviets, the Colossus computer has solved the false-submarine problem *and* has located Deep Throat. When the Soviet president comes on the line, the president of the United States begins slowly, "Dimitri, I think there's something you should know . . ."

16

Have the Europeans Gone Crazy?
Nuclear War: What's In It for the Europeans?

Two nightmares haunt the defense ministers of Western Europe: a vision of Soviet tanks and troops pouring across the North German Plain, and the awful prospect of the United States and the Soviet Union slugging it out with nuclear weapons—but only in Europe. Americans don't always understand this. The American government has been worrying about a Soviet attack in Europe since 1945, but the American people rarely focus on this prospect. The Soviet Union is too far away—thousands of miles across the Atlantic or Pacific Ocean, or over the North Pole. A conventional attack on the United States would be impossible, and until recently the prospect of a nuclear attack seemed remote.

But in Europe things look different. Russian troops are right there—in East Germany, in Poland, in Czechoslovakia. The border is marked by barbed wire, guard towers, mine fields, and armed men who don't hesitate to shoot down refugees trying to escape to the West. In the late 1940s, when Europe was still recovering from the devastation of World War II, fear of Russia was at a high pitch. The Russians occupied all of Eastern Europe, including Austria. Soviet armies were immense. Local Communist parties were large and active. So Europe turned to the United States for protection from the first nightmare—a Russian invasion—and thereby created the second nightmare—the potential for a nuclear war in Europe.

The History of Nuclear Weapons In Europe

U.S. nuclear weapons have been in Western Europe since 1948, when the U.S. flew some over in B-29s as a gesture of resolve at the time of the Berlin blockade. The B-29s, and the B-36s which followed, could reach the Soviet Union; they were meant to deter a conventional attack on Europe by the forty-odd divisions of Soviet troops which had been stationed in Eastern Europe since 1945. American nuclear weapons in Western Europe also had a second purpose. Since it was anticipated that any nuclear war in Europe would quickly escalate to full-scale war, this weaponry represented a political as well as military tie between the defense of our NATO allies and our own security. NATO's threat of a large-scale nuclear attack ("massive retaliation") against the Soviet Union stood as a deterrent against a Soviet invasion of Western Europe, just as it was a deterrent against a Soviet attack on the United States. In short, as the North Atlantic Treaty requires, an attack on any of us would be considered an attack on all of us.

This linkage was modified in the early 1960s when the Kennedy administration introduced the doctrine of "flexible response," a concept intended to offer an American president a range of responsive alternatives between surrender and all-out nuclear war. If the Russians launched an all-out attack, that was one thing. But what if they launched a "little" attack? Kennedy wanted the ability to make a "little" response. As a practical matter, this came down to better, "more usable" tactical nuclear weapons—short-range missiles, fighter-bombers, artillery shells, land mines, and so forth. We weren't expecting a

Soviet attack, exactly, but we wanted them to know it would be resisted if it came.

This new doctrine of "flexible response" tripled the number of nuclear warheads in NATO forces to seven thousand between 1960 and 1968. While some Europeans saw this as a comforting demonstration of U.S. willingness to risk nuclear war in their defense, many others saw it as a move to separate, or "decouple," Western European and American security. We both hoped to avoid war totally, but if war came anyway, these Europeans wanted to be sure the U.S. did not attempt to confine the war, especially a nuclear war, to European soil. Flexible response seemed to make such geographical limitation possible.

NATO and the Warsaw Pact had a rough balance in intermediate-range (1,000- to 3,000-mile) systems in the 1960s and 1970s. The Soviet Union had deployed about six hundred medium- and intermediate-range ballistic missiles (SS-4s and SS-5s)—the same missiles it tried to base in Cuba in the early 1960s. By the end of the 1970s Britain and France had each built four ballistic missile submarines—a total of sixty-four launch tubes—and France had deployed eighteen intermediate-range ballistic missiles in silos. In addition, the United States based about seventy-five long-range F-111 bombers in England and assigned several hundred Poseidon SLBM warheads to NATO control in the early 1970s. But in the late 1970s this rough balance suddenly began to tilt in favor of the Soviets when they introduced the Backfire bomber and the SS-20, a 2,500-mile three-warhead MIRVed ballistic missile.

In 1977, as the Soviets began deploying the SS-20s and modernizing their battlefield nuclear weapons, NATO began to discuss the introduction of the neutron bomb into Western Europe as a tactical nuclear weapon for use primarily against the superior Soviet tank forces. The neutron bomb, like any other nuclear weapon (Chapter 2), produces a devastating shock wave, thermal radiation, and other effects. It is unique, however, in also producing a large amount of neutron radiation—about ten times as much as other nuclear weapons of similar size. Neutron bombs kill people—tank crews, for example—but don't do quite as much damage to physical objects.

Many Western Europeans—and Americans— thought the neutron bomb was evidence of increased American willingness to fight a nuclear war in Europe, and substantial public opposition to the weapon ensued. After a difficult series of exchanges within the alliance, President Carter eventually decided not to proceed with the planned deployment of neutron bombs. In the process, relations between the United States and its NATO allies were severely strained.

The New Missiles

The 1979 NATO proposal called for the deployment of 108 Pershing IIs and 464 Tomahawks in West Germany, England, Belgium, Italy, and the Netherlands.

The Pershing IIs, with a range of 1,000 miles, would replace the 108 currently deployed Pershing I missiles, whose 400-mile range is too short to reach across East Germany and Poland to the Soviet Union. (The Germans have an additional 72 Pershing I missiles whose nuclear warheads can only be armed by U.S. authority.)

The Tomahawk ground-launched cruise missiles, with a range of 1,500 miles, would be an entirely new deployment. Ironically, in the early 1970s, the ground-launched cruise missiles were considered a "bargaining chip" to be traded away in SALT II negotiations with the Soviet Union.* It was thought that no one wanted to deploy such missiles. But the emergence of

---

*Sea-launched cruise missiles (from submarines and surface ships) were also considered a "bargaining chip" in this period.

the Soviet SS-20 changed this view. The Tomahawk can strike at the Soviet Union with considerable accuracy from as far away as Sicily and Great Britain. Its ability to fly at low altitudes—less than fifty feet over flat terrain and a few hundred feet over rough terrain—allows it to penetrate defenses. Initially, the U.S. military wanted 1,500 Tomahawks, while the Europeans—for political reasons—specified no more than 200. The 464 Tomahawks eventually settled on were a compromise. Although the total proposed deployment of 572 missiles was not sized by reference to any particular set of targets, the force was seen as strengthening NATO's ability to attack a broad range of military targets in the Soviet Union.

The European Battlefield

The new American missiles were intended to convey NATO unity and resolve in the face of the increased nuclear threat posed by the SS-20s—about two hundred fifty of which had been deployed by the end of 1981.

As NATO moved toward the scheduled 1983/4 deployment of the new missiles, Europeans became uneasy. Because of their location, some West Germans feared that their country would become the principal East-West battleground for a war limited to the European continent. These fears were heightened by the continued inability of NATO military planners and political leaders to spell out in detail how, when, where, and why the decisions would be made to move up each rung of the escalation ladder from conventional weapons to short-range tactical nuclear weapons and to the proposed new longer-range Tomahawk and Pershing missiles capable of reaching the Soviet Union. NATO already had six thousand tactical nuclear weapons, enough to promise major damage and death in Central Europe in the event of war. It also had the capability to attack targets in the Soviet Union with the Poseidon warheads assigned to the NATO commander and the British submarine and bomber forces.

The European Disarmament Movement

European public resistance to NATO plans to install the new Tomahawk and Pershing II missiles began to emerge immediately after the announcement of the decision. The NATO governments, anticipating such a reaction, had insisted that the deployment decision be accompanied by a "parallel track" of U.S.-Soviet negotiation on limitations on European nuclear missiles.*

It was not enough to contain opposition to the missile decision which quickly spread across Europe. Its intensity and its breadth across European countries and classes caught both government officials and most observers altogether by surprise. The vehemence of public objection to the plan is attributable to several causes.

- Fear that a "limited" nuclear war meant a nuclear war limited to Europe, heightened by public statements by President Reagan on the possibility of limiting a nuclear war to Europe.
- U.S. failure to ratify SALT II and the collapse of détente, which to the Europeans implied that little was to be expected of new Soviet-American arms control efforts—especially when the new U.S. administration frequently stated its determination to improve its defenses *before* initiating serious arms control negotiations.
- Existence of a generation gap between younger demonstrators, who had never experienced the

---

*A planning session for these negotiations took place in the fall of 1980, and the negotiations formally began in December 1981.

cold war, and their elders, now running the Western European governments, who had lived through the late 1940s and early 1950s when fear of Russia was at its greatest intensity.

- Agitation by the Soviet Union and by socialists and Communists in Europe to oppose the planned Tomahawk and Pershing deployments.
- Revival by the Reagan administration of the neutron bomb, manifest in a decision in August 1981 to stockpile the weapon in the United States for possible future use in Europe.
- In the specific case of Great Britain, a Labour party stand favoring unilateral nuclear disarmament.

The Long-Term Significance of European Disarmament Effects

As opposition to the Pershing and Tomahawk missiles has spread, it has broadened to include attacks on the American presence in Europe and the whole NATO policy of flexible response and nuclear deterrence. The result has been a range of dramatic proposals such as limiting nuclear warheads strictly to tactical weapons, creation of nuclear-free zones without any warheads, and even unilateral nuclear disarmament of the entire region.

Support for these proposals stems partly from popular anger both at European governments, for having routinely made major decisions about defense without consulting the general public, and at the United States, for assuming that it can dictate NATO policy almost unilaterally. Political and military leaders throughout NATO openly admit that in this regard they have mishandled policy decisions.

Several lessons are to be drawn from these developments. First, the United States may lead NATO, but it can't tell it what to do indefinitely. Second, the European public is far from certain it is protected by American nuclear weapons. Third, careless handling of these problems could lead to NATO's collapse—especially if Europe is allowed to go on thinking the U.S. is a kind of "nuclear cowboy" itching for a fight. Fourth, the United States *needs* its European allies; the alliance helps to protect all its members. Finally, there is the lesson of the failure of European governments to maintain contact and communication with their citizens on vital security issues—a problem the United States may yet have to confront.

17

Guess Who's Got the Bomb Now?: The Problem of Nuclear Weapons Proliferation

In June of 1981, the Israeli Air Force made the most dramatic public statement to date on the subject of nuclear weapons proliferation—the acquisition of nuclear weapons by additional countries. Just before sundown, Israeli jets flew across Jordan and Saudi Arabia and into Iraq, where they bombed and destroyed Iraq's Osirak nuclear reactor. Israel made no attempt to deny the raid but insisted it had had no choice. Iraq was planning to build an atomic bomb, Tel Aviv said, and Israel was its target.

According to the dictionary, *proliferation* means a rapid increase or spread of something. In 1945 only a handful of atomic scientists worried about it. Military authorities, including General Leslie Groves, who had run the Manhattan Project during the war, thought it might take the Russians twenty years or more to build a bomb of their own. It took them four. Since then we have been worrying about proliferation.

Indeed, no aspect of the nuclear threat has received more attention than proliferation. It has been the subject of endless negotiation, analysis in the professional literature, debate in the UN, and plain worry in the capitals of what has come to be called the Nuclear Club. At the moment, the club has six acknowledged members: the United States, Russia, Britain, France,

China, and India. All except India have tested both fission and fusion, or hydrogen, bombs. Most experts agree that two other nations—Israel and South Africa—probably have, or at the very least could quickly make, nuclear weapons. Many other nations could build a bomb, too, if they chose to do so. The United States has tried hard to discourage them, and Israel, as we have seen, did not stop at words.

Nuclear Proliferation: So What?

Why are we so concerned about nuclear proliferation? Don't we claim that nuclear weapons have helped to prevent war between the United States and the Soviet Union? Why shouldn't other nations protect themselves with nuclear weapons as well? Don't nuclear weapons make war "impossible"?

The nuclear nations are not altogether honest in their answers to these questions. The truth of the matter is that we built the weapons before we really knew what they would be good for. After we had them, we tried to explain *why* we had them. The answer was deterrence. The fact that we urge other nations not to depend on nuclear weapons in this way—and urge very strenuously—suggests that we have mixed feelings about how safe they make us.

There *is* an argument against proliferation. Think of the world as a Western town. What would protect the citizens best—a reliable marshal with a few well-disciplined deputies, or every man carrying his own gun? The argument against nuclear proliferation is a simple one: the greater number of nations with nuclear weapons, the greater chance of nuclear war—including all-out war between the United States and the Soviet Union.

The problem is the law of averages—the number of combinations. Think how many nations in the world are at odds with their neighbors: North Korea and South Korea, Pakistan and India, Iran and Iraq, Israel and the Arab states, South Africa and its neighbors. A complete list would be a long one. In several cases, these nations have already engaged in full-scale conventional wars—and have by no means settled their differences. Indeed, many remain passionate enemies. What would happen if, in a future war, one of these nations used a nuclear weapon? The victim would be certain to respond, if it could, in kind. And what about the involvement of the superpowers? Recent history and common sense suggest that the superpowers could hardly stand aside while their allies were trying to destroy each other. The United States and the Soviet Union could suddenly find themselves involved in a conflict in which nuclear weapons are already being used—the first step up the escalation ladder which everyone seeks to avoid.

A second reason to worry about nuclear proliferation focuses on terrorism. An increase in the number of nuclear weapons development programs, especially in less stable countries, would make it easier for terrorist groups to get their hands on the necessary materials to build a bomb of their own. They might even be able to steal an existing bomb. A terrorist group with a bomb could threaten a whole city with destruction if its demands were not met.

A third awful possibility is that nuclear weapons could get into the hands of a national leader whose sanity is open to question. In this sense, we are far more dependent on the rationality of national leaders for preventing nuclear war than we want to admit. Do you want Qaddafi to have the bomb?

A fourth source of worry is simple humanitarian concern for the destructive capacity of nuclear weapons, coupled with the belief that other nations might be more willing to use them. This is, of course, a bit of a "Father Knows Best" attitude, but one which probably reflects an element of truth. We don't want anyone to suffer the consequences of a nuclear war—small or large.

Finally, there is alarm that our luck might just run out. As each new member state joins the exclusive Nuclear Club, the chances of a nuclear weapon going off increase. A nation with a nuclear weapon is a kind of wild card. When the deck is filled with wild cards, it becomes impossible for the game to be orderly—or rational.

The History of Nonproliferation Efforts: Not a Great Report Card

Following the first atomic explosion in 1945, the United States went to great lengths to keep its "secret." No other nation, not even our wartime ally Great Britain, was told how to build a bomb. A law passed in 1946 declared the certain information was "born secret"—classified even if it was discovered by a high-school student in his own home. But the principal secret of the atomic bomb—that one could actually be built—was out. The Soviet Union exploded its first atomic bomb in 1949. By 1953 Great Britain had exploded its first atomic bomb and the Soviet Union and the United States had both tested hydrogen bombs.

By this time it was clear that nuclear weapons proliferation was going to be a problem, especially since many nations wanted to build commercial nuclear power plants. Power plants produce plutonium, and plutonium can be used to build a bomb. To deal with this problem, President Eisenhower proposed the "Atoms for Peace" program, which offered to help other nations build reactors so long as they adopted safeguards to prevent the diversion of nuclear materials from peaceful to military purposes. In 1957 the United Nations created the International Atomic Energy Agency (IAEA) to administer the proposed safeguards. However, there was only a blurry distinction between "peaceful" and "military" uses of nuclear materials. The United States was not the only country worried that nuclear power plants would be used to create bomb-grade material. Negotiations for a treaty to deal with the problem began under UN auspices in 1966, and two years later the Nonproliferation Treaty (NPT) was signed.

In essence, the NPT asks nations without nuclear weapons to accept a trade-off: in return for a commitment for forgo nuclear weapons, they would receive full cooperation and assistance in developing peaceful civilian uses of nuclear energy from the nations that do have nuclear weapons. Signatories are expected to accept inspection of their facilities by international teams from the IAEA. The treaty also commits nuclear weapons states to undertake arms control negotiations leading to "cessation of the nuclear arms race at an early date."

So far, 123 countries have signed the NPT. Two nuclear weapons states, France and China, have not signed. Israel and South Africa, who deny they have nuclear weapons although many experts think they do, have also not signed. Several other states believed to be working on the bomb—Pakistan, for example—have not signed, either.

Who's Next?

The fact is that dozens of other nations could build nuclear weapons within the next ten years, should they decide to do so. A rough list of current and potential Nuclear Club members is shown in Table 17.1. It should be noted that some of those nations in the "Probably Won't Try" category might change their minds. For others, like Poland and Japan, development of nuclear weapons would be politically impossible. The actual list of new club members over the next ten years will be determined by a combination of individual desire, technical know-how, political events, and the effectiveness of nonproliferation efforts by the UN and individual nations like the United

TABLE 17.1.
The Nuclear Club—Current and Potential Members

Current Members	Probable Current Members	Could Be Members in Ten Years		
		Probably Won't Try	Might Try	Probably Will Try
United States (1945)	Israel	Australia	Argentina	Iraq
Soviet Union (1949)	South Africa	Austria	Brazil	Libya
Great Britain (1952)		Belgium	South Korea	Pakistan
France (1960)		Canada	Taiwan	
China (1964)		Czechoslovakia		
India (1974)		Denmark		
		East Germany		
		Finland		
		Italy		
		Japan		
		Netherlands		
		Norway		
		Poland		
		Rumania		
		Spain		
		Sweden		
		Switzerland		
		West Germany		
		Yugoslavia		

States and the Soviet Union. There are good reasons for hoping the Nuclear Club will not grow, but most analysts believe it will.

How to Do It

You might wonder how nonnuclear states would get the material with which to build a bomb. For countries which have little domestic nuclear technology, the steps—which involve varying degrees of difficulty—are

1. Purchase a nuclear reactor either for research or power production from the United States, Canada, France, Germany, or one of the other half dozen nations that have the capability to build such reactors and are often eager to sell them.
2. Acquire fuel for the reactor from a fuel supplier nation like the United States or France.
3. Secretly process or refine the fuel to separate weapons-grade fissionable materials (uranium 235 or plutonium 239; see Chapter 2).
4. Use the fissionable material to assemble a weapon—the easiest part.

Nonproliferation involves a real dilemma. In view of many nonnuclear weapon states, under the Nonproliferation Treaty, nations which have nuclear weapons are *obligated* to sell research reactors and power reactors to those that don't. Once a country is in possession of a reactor, there is no easy way to stop it from siphoning off the weapons-grade fissionable material which, because it is required for fusion (hydrogen) bombs as well as for fission (atomic) bombs, is the focus of nonproliferation policy efforts. The difficulties of effective inspection become clear when you consider that building a simple bomb requires only about 10 to 20 kilograms (22 to 44 pounds) of plutonium 239 or 15 to 20 kilograms (33 to 66 pounds) of highly enriched uranium 235.

Research reactors of the kind often maintained by the physics departments of universities pose a particular problem in this regard because the fuel they use contains a high proportion of fissionable material—uranium 235. This makes it easier to refine the fuel to a quality (e.g., 97 percent uranium U-235) suitable for weapons. Fortunately, at least in the case of uranium fuel, the refining process, called enrichment, involves complex and expensive methods not readily available to a would-be illicit weapon builder. Nevertheless, the export of research reactors and their fuel is closely monitored.

Nuclear power reactors present a problem because of the plutonium produced as their by-product. Only about 3 percent of the uranium fuel used in a typical commercial reactor is fissionable uranium 235. The balance is uranium 238, some of which is converted to fissionable plutonium in the power-production process. A modern nuclear power plant that generates 500 million watts of electricity—enough to meet the needs of a city of half a million people—produces about a hundred pounds of plutonium 239 over a two-year period—enough for five to ten simple weapons. Fortunately, the fuel rods in which the plutonium is embedded are highly radioactive and difficult to handle. Unfortunately, dealing with them is not impossible.

As shown in the simplified fuel cycle in Figure 17.1, the reprocessing of spent fuel involves separation of the material into plutonium, uranium, and waste products. The uranium can be returned to an enrichment facility which raises its uranium 235 level to the 3 percent necessary for use in so-called light water reactors. This uranium is relatively benign, since it would have to undergo enrichment to over 90 percent pure uranium 235 before it could be used to make a nuclear weapon. The plutonium obtained from reprocessing, however, can be used directly in nuclear weapons.

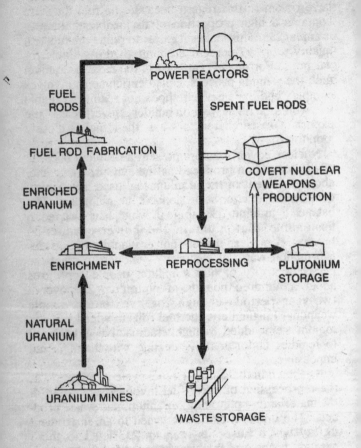

POWER REACTORS

FUEL RODS

SPENT FUEL RODS

FUEL ROD FABRICATION

COVERT NUCLEAR WEAPONS PRODUCTION

ENRICHED URANIUM

ENRICHMENT

REPROCESSING

PLUTONIUM STORAGE

NATURAL URANIUM

URANIUM MINES

WASTE STORAGE

FIGURE 17.1
The Nuclear Fuel Cycle

As can be seen in Figure 17.1, there are two prime points in the cycle where plutonium might be diverted for use in a nuclear explosive. Although it is difficult to divert and transport such dangerous material without detection, a nation or terrorist group might attempt to do so. Diversion of enriched uranium also poses danger, but this problem is not nearly as great as that of plutonium.

Perspectives on a Difficult Problem

Given the existence of a nonproliferation treaty signed by 123 countries and an international agency specifically organized to administer safeguards against misuse of weapons-related materials, it may seem hard to understand why so many additional nations appear to be well on their way to developing the capacity to produce nuclear weapons. The fact of the matter is that the NPT and IAEA policy procedures contain many loopholes.

As previously noted, an NPT country can do just about anything short of actually testing a weapon without violating the treaty. Even when violations are detected, the IAEA has no power to impose penalties, and it is not allowed to inspect any facilities or materials except those openly declared by the country. And last, but perhaps most important, it is extremely difficult to prove that a so-called peaceful nuclear explosion (the term used by India to describe its 1974 test) is actually intended for military purposes. The concept of a peaceful nuclear explosion is, of course, somewhat of a contradiction in terms (even though at one time the use of nuclear weapons for mining and canal building was considered). Yet the relatively lax framework of the NPT and IAEA makes such claims difficult to contest.

Although existing structures have contributed to slowing the development of nuclear weapons, the loopholes in the current system will only begin to close if there is (1) greater commitment on the part of suppliers to restrict the highly sensitive materials and technology provided to other countries; (2) tighter restriction of the technical information necessary for nuclear weapons production; (3) better safeguards on all materials and reactors, some of which are not covered by IAEA inspections today; and (4) provision of real penalties that hurt for nations violating treaty terms. If none of these policies and mechanisms are implemented, we will eventually all be living in the nuclear-age equivalent of an Old West town where everybody carries a gun.

EPILOGUE

On a Clear Day You Can See the End of the World: Finding Our Way out of the Current Dilemma

You now know at least as much about nuclear weapons and nuclear war as any United States president. You might not be in possession of some of the closely guarded details of how American forces operate or the day-to-day intelligence on Soviet activities, but you understand the "big picture" on which virtually all nuclear weapons and nuclear war decisions are based.

You are also now sufficiently well informed to comprehend the strengths and weaknesses of the arguments put forth by the "experts," and you can now personally evaluate the views of the individuals and groups who span the spectrum of opinion on nuclear weapons and nuclear war—from the advocates of disarmament and weapons freezes to those who would accelerate the building of weapons to keep ahead (or get ahead) of the Soviet Union.

You now should be familiar enough with the essential technical aspects of nuclear weapons and their delivery systems that you, too, can judge such questions as whether we should have a new B-1 bomber, wait for Stealth, or try another scheme; whether we should put M-X missiles in old fixed silos, in a massive "shell game" in Nevada/Utah, or abandon the plan altogether. You may not know the subtleties of the new weapons technologies, but you do have sufficient knowledge to probe for basic explanations of how things work.

Finally, and most important, you should have the confidence to go beyond this book, to learn more about those features of nuclear weapons, nuclear war, and Soviet-American relations about which you have a special concern, and, indeed, to become something of an expert in your own right. We hope we have stimulated your desire to take the initiative and say to yourself, "I can and will have a role in a dialogue about the security of myself, my family, my community, and my country."

We Can Do It

One of the remarkable characteristics of the American people throughout history is our "can do" attitude—our sense that we control our personal and national destiny. This distinctive American attitude—a combination of philosophical optimism, day-to-day pragmatism, and historical experience—has been with us from the earliest settlements at Plymouth and Jamestown through the Revolutionary and Civil wars, the building of the urban metropolis, the settlement of the West, a disastrous depression, two world wars, and the conquest of space. These challenges were not easy for individual Americans or for the nation as a whole. But we prevailed in all of them.

Preventing nuclear war is a tremendous challenge which involves not only the integration of the intentions and capabilities of our own nation with those of our enemies and allies, but also an integration of the threat of nuclear war with our everyday life. Yet there is nothing in any of the parts of the problem which suggests that the problem is insoluble. In particular, there is nothing to justify a fatalistic view that The Bombs will come regardless of the actions of ourselves or anyone else.

We met those earlier challenges by integrating the individual efforts of hundreds, thousands, and eventually millions of people, acting as heads of governments and heads of households, working in trenches, kitchens, fields, and factories—thinking, leading, building, voting. In this same way we must meet the challenge presented by the threat of nuclear war.

The American philosopher Ralph Waldo Emerson once wrote, "It was a thought that built this whole portentous war establishment, and a thought shall melt it away." He was writing in the last century, but his words are even more to the point today. The danger we face is of our own making. Nuclear weapons don't have to be like the weather—something everybody talks about but nobody does anything about. We—Americans and Russians alike—got ourselves into this situation, and we can get ourselves out.

So What Can I Do?

So what can *I* do? We have heard this question again and again in the months since the inception of Ground Zero. Here is what we have told people all over the country.

- *Be confident.* You can understand the issues and arguments surrounding the subject of nuclear war. The information you need is available, not all hidden under a "top secret" stamp.
- *Try your wings.* Tell your family, friends, and co-workers how you think and feel about nuclear war. Be candid about your fears and hopes. Explain what you think we can do about it. As the Bible recommends, don't hide your light under a bushel.
- *Speak out.* Don't keep your thoughts to yourself. The letters to the editor section of your local newspaper is an excellent forum for you to speak

out on any issue which affects you or your community. Write to your elected representatives in Washington. Don't forget that they work for you. Tell them that you're worried about the number of nuclear weapons in the world, that you hope they'll try to do something about it.

- *Think big*. There is no limit to what people can do when they work together. You aren't the only one in your community worried about nuclear war. Look for the others in your local church or community groups. If you can't find anyone already working on the problem, start a group of your own.

- *Don't give up*. It has taken us nearly forty years to get into the present mess. We won't get out of it overnight. The world takes time to come around.

- *Don't wait for the answer*. No one has *the* solution to the problem of nuclear weapons. You don't have to figure out every last detail before you write a letter to the editor. It's your expression of concern that will touch other people. Remember that the world's leaders don't know what to do either. If they did, we would not find ourselves in this situation.

A New Road

Early in this century, the American poet Robert Frost wrote a poem entitled "The Road Not Taken," which closes with these words:

> Two roads diverged in a wood, and I—
> I took the one less traveled by,
> And that has made all the difference.

We, the American people, today find ourselves traveling at an accelerating speed on a road that is growing increasingly obscure and dangerous. This is the road

we have chosen—to make ourselves safe with more
and more nuclear weapons, to caution potential enemies through intimidation and fear. We aren't the only
ones on the road. The Soviet Union is on it, too. So are
our allies and their allies—and, like it or not, so are the
rest of the nations of the world.

But the road we're on is no longer taking us where
we want to go. We do not feel safer. Indeed, we have
never been more threatened than we are now. It is
inevitable that we should ask ourselves, our friends,
and our enemies alike: Is there no safer road?

In the ancient world, Rome and Carthage were
bitter enemies. They fought until Carthage was utterly
defeated, her cities pulled down stone by stone, her
fields sowed with salt. But it does not have to end that
way. For hundreds of years, until 1815, France and
Britain were enemies. But then they made peace, and
they have been friends and allies ever since.

From 1941 until 1945 the United States was locked
in war with Japan and Germany. We killed hundreds of
thousands of their soldiers and citizens, sank their
ships, and destroyed their cities. But then, within a
few years, we became friends and allies. War does not
have to breed only war. Enmity does not have to last
forever. We have a choice.

A few years ago the late president of Egypt, Anwar
Sadat, looked down the road his nation was on. He
saw only death and destruction, war upon war. He saw
nuclear bombs on Cairo, on Alexandria, on the Aswan
Dam—suffering and impoverishment without end.
And so he led his people on a different road—to
Jerusalem and Camp David—and changed forever the
political landscape of the Middle East. With Mena-
chem Begin of Israel he shared a Nobel Prize for
peace, but it was peace itself which was his true
reward.

Someday an American president may look down the
road we're on and see the prospect of nuclear weapons

raining down on Washington, on New York, on Los Angeles, on Green Bay, Wisconsin, and Tucumcari, New Mexico—on all we have hoped and built. He will have to decide: do we stay on that road, or take another?

He can't make that decision alone. He will need support and encouragement from us. He will need to know that we are prepared to take another road—a road that leads away from nuclear war. It is our choice as much as it is his. Are you ready to take a road less traveled by—and make the difference?

APPENDIX A

Twenty Questions about Nuclear War You've Been Afraid to Ask

1. If there were a nuclear war with the Soviet Union, would the president of the United States survive?

Answer: Probably not.

It is almost certain that any large-scale Soviet attack on the United States would include an attack on Washington in order to disrupt the structure for commanding U.S. military forces. If the attack were "a bolt from the blue" or if it occurred in the early stages of a crisis, the president would probably be in Washington and would be killed along with his cabinet, the Congress, and the Joint Chiefs of Staff.

While in principle the president might, upon satellite warning of an attack, run from his office, get on a helicopter, and escape the Washington area, in practice it seems highly unlikely that this would work. The time it takes for a helicopter to get to the White House (three to five minutes) and to escape the area (five to ten minutes) does not compare favorably to the time (about seven to ten minutes) between satellite warning and arrival of a ballistic missile from a submarine. If the attack were from a Soviet submarine-launched cruise missile (unlikely now but possible in the future), there would be no warning at all.

In an escalating crisis, the president would essentially have three choices: (1) remain in Washington, (2) get on board a specially equipped airplane and randomly fly around the country, or (3) go to a secret underground command post. The argument for his remaining in Washington (as Kennedy did in the Cuban missile crisis) is that his departure could panic the nation or lead to an escalation in the crisis. The special airplane, the National Emergency Airborne Command Post (NEACP—often referred to as Kneecap), is a 747 which can, in principle, stay aloft for a long as three or four days as long as refueling is available (oil supply problems necessitate landing after this period). During a large-scale attack on the United States, tankers for repeated refueling might well not be available. In such a situation the president could, in principle, fly to Central or South America to take refuge. The final alternative of a secret command post is attractive but only if there is assurance that the Soviets do not know of its existence. There are a number of such underground shelters for government officials in the mountains west of Washington, but the Soviets almost certainly have them targeted. While a nuclear weapon targeted on such shelters might not immediately kill the occupants inside, it would almost certainly seal up the entrance and create an eventual underground tomb.

2. **What would happen in the United States if the president and his designated successors left Washington, D.C., during a crisis?**

Answer: No one knows. It is possible that such action, which certainly would be detected and publicized, would lead to mass evacuation of U.S. cities, mass purchasing of food and medical supplies, and so forth. What do you think you would do?

3. **If Washington is attacked and it is clear that the president and other high-ranking officials have been killed, how will we know who is the highest-ranking survivor?**

Answer: We won't. With the disruption of communications that would result, it could be days or even weeks before it is known who is the new "president." As a consequence, the war will be conducted by a few military officers who are aloft around the clock in special airplanes. One of these, called Looking Glass, is based in Omaha, Nebraska, and is commanded by an air force general. This airplane will direct U.S. ICBMs and bombers. Other airplanes, called Tacamo, serve the same role in the Atlantic and Pacific for U.S. ballistic missile submarines. When these airplanes are forced to land for a lack of fuel (say, in five to ten hours), coordinated military action will cease unless they can be refueled—which seems unlikely. All subsequent military action will be in the hands of individual commanders whose units survive the initial exchanges.

4. How do U.S. nuclear forces know when to launch an attack?

Answer: The president is always accompanied by a military officer who carries a small black bag (called "the football" because of its size and shape) containing the codes for launching U.S. nuclear forces. If the president wants to order an attack, he picks a particular attack option and the military officer passes the code to U.S. forces through what is called an Emergency Action Message (EAM). For example, if he picks an option which calls for an all-out attack on the Soviet military, economic, and leadership targets, the numerical code for that option for that day is passed to U.S. military commanders. They in turn match this number with the numbers in their code books and follow the appropriate instructions.

For ICBMs and bombers, the message to launch a retaliatory attack would probably go through the Looking Glass airplane. For submarines, the message would probably go through the Tacamo aircraft.

5. How does the United States detect the launch of Soviet missiles?

Answer: The most important U.S. missile attack warning system is called the Defense Support Program (DSP) satellite system. The system consists of three satellites in so-called stationary equatorial orbits (i.e., the satellites are at a 22,000-mile altitude, which means they go around the earth at the same rate the earth turns and thus always maintain the same position over the equator). The one satellite in the Eastern Hemisphere observes missile launches from Soviet (and Chinese) territory. The other two are positioned in the Western Hemisphere and serve to detect SLBM launches from the Atlantic and Pacific. These satellites scan the earth every ten seconds, looking for strong infrared signals from the rocket plumes behind the missile booster. By plotting the tracks from these plumes as the booster burns, a rough idea of the direction of flight (e.g., toward the eastern, midwestern, or western part of the United States) can be obtained.

The DSP satellites provide about twenty-five minutes of warning for an ICBM attack and seven to ten minutes' warning for an SLBM attack. (ICBM flight time is about thirty minutes. SLBM flight time is about ten to twenty minutes, depending on range.)

We also have a backup system of Ballistic Missile Early Warning System (BMEWS) radars in Alaska, Greenland, and England for detecting ICBM attacks. The BMEWS radar detect the ICBMs about fifteen minutes after launch (or fifteen minutes before impact). BMEWS provides an accurate estimate (within a few tens of miles) of where the missile warheads will land.

We also have a backup system for detecting SLBM attacks called PAVE PAWS. It consists of four radars on the East and West coasts of the United States. This system also provides accurate estimates of the intended targets and about five to ten minutes of warning time.

6. Could the Soviets destroy the systems we use for providing warning of a missile attack, and if so, what would we do?

Answer: Our principal missile attack warning system, the Defense Support Program (DSP) satellite system, is currently invulnerable. The three satellites in this system are at a 22,000-mile altitude—well beyond the range of Soviet antisatellite systems. However, the Soviets could destroy our backup warning systems— the land-based BMEWS radar system for detecting ICBM attacks and the PAVE PAWS radar system for detecting SLBM attacks.

It is possible that by the end of the decade all of our warning systems, including the DSP satellite system, would be vulnerable. If all of these systems were destroyed by the Soviets but no other attack took place, it would put us in a very difficult position, since we are critically dependent on these systems to get our bombers off the ground and other actions. If you were the president, what would you do if these systems were suddenly destroyed?

7. Have there ever been any false alarms where our warning systems indicated a missile attack which never materialized?

Answer: Yes, several.

The best-known occurred in the mid-1960s shortly after the Ballistic Missile Early Warning System (BMEWS) was completed. One day, one of the sites indicated that a massive missile raid on the United States was taking place. Because the system was fairly new, the commander of the installation cautioned that it might be a false alarm—which of course it was. Later it was determined that what the radar had seen was the rising of the *moon*. The radar signals had gone all the way to the moon and bounced back. Apparently the computer program in the BMEWS computer had never taken into account this possibility and the moon had for the first time come into the field of view of the radar. Imagine—World War III almost starting because of the moon rising.

In a 1979 incident at the Colorado Springs headquarters of the North American Air Defense Command (NORAD), a computer processing data from the satellite missile warning system failed—as frequently happens with computers. The incoming satellite data were rerouted to a backup computer, which also failed. Incoming data were then rerouted to a second backup computer, which after a short period of operation indicated a massive missile raid on the United States. Apparently a practice tape which had been used for testing air force personnel had been inadvertently left on one of the backup computer tape drives.

Within a few minutes, this error was discovered, but not before the false information had been transmitted to U.S. military installations around the country.

In June of 1980, the computer display system at U.S. Air Force Strategic Air Command (SAC) headquarters in Omaha, Nebraska, indicated a large number of SLBM launches against the United States. (This is one of the military installations which receive warning system data directly from NORAD.) A check with the NORAD command post in Colorado found no indication of any SLBM launches on its equipment. Eventually the computer display at SAC cleared and the situation returned to normal. However, in the initial confusion, the SAC duty officer directed all alert B-52 crews (over a hundred airplanes) to go to their aircraft and start their engines should a quick takeoff be necessary in order to survive. None of the B-52s actually took off.

On June 6, as SAC sought to determine the source of the malfunction, the incident was repeated—this time with the indication of a number of ICBM launches. Later it was determined that a "faulty integrated circuit in a communications multiplexer", i.e., a faulty computer chip the size of a fingernail, was responsible for the incidents.

While there have been a few other minor incidents, those described above have been the most serious. How does it make you feel about the idea of launching U.S. ICBMs when our warning systems indicate an attack? Does it make you wonder about the Soviet warning systems?

8. **What does the commander of a U.S. ballistic missile submarine do if suddenly all communications from the U.S. cease? Does he launch his missiles?**

Answer: Hopefully, a U.S. submarine commander would at least get a final message that an attack on the U.S. had taken place, even in a situation where the president and other top commanders are killed immediately so that no specific order to launch a retaliatory attack is provided. In such circumstances, he and other commanders would follow preset plans for launching a coordinated retaliatory attack.

If there is no message at all, as would be the case if the Tacamo aircraft and all other communications links were immediately destroyed, the commander and his officers would presumably have to assume that the U.S. had been attacked and respond accordingly, again according to preset plans.

9. **How many of our ICBMs would survive a Soviet attack? What about our ballistic missile submarines? What about our bombers?**

Answer: If the Soviet Union attacked the U.S. ICBM force today, about 30 to 40 percent of our 1,052 ICBMs would survive. By 1986 the number of surviving ICBMs would probably be about 10 to 20 percent.

We maintain about half of our nearly forty ballistic missile submarines (SSBNs) at sea at all times. In a crisis, the number at sea would increase to 70 to 80 percent of the force. We are confident that all of the at-sea SSBNs would survive an attack. Those in port are highly vulnerable and would undoubtedly be destroyed.

We maintain between 100 and 150 of our 350 B-52 bombers on "alert" status at all times. For the foreseeable future, we are confident that almost all of these alert B-52 bombers would get off the ground and survive a Soviet attack. In a crisis, an additional 100 to 150 B-52s would be on alert. Most of these would be likely to survive, but the last few might be caught by an SLBM attack on their bases.

10. How many of the six thousand U.S. nuclear weapons in Europe would survive a Soviet attack?

Answer: All of our nuclear forces in Europe are vulnerable to a "bolt from the blue" attack. We have about fifty Pershing I missiles and about seventy fighter-bombers on what is called Quick Reaction Alert (QRA), but even these forces would not survive a "bolt from the blue" attack. The QRA Pershings need about an hour of warning to disperse, and the QRA aircraft need about fifteen minutes. The Pershing II and ground-launched cruise missiles planned for deployment in 1983 would have essentially the same vulnerability as today's Pershing Is.

11. How many Americans would die if the Soviet Union attacked only the 1,052 U.S. silo-based ICBMs?

Answer: Between two and twenty million, depending on such factors as weather conditions, the yield of the Soviet weapons, and the height at which they are exploded. Almost all of the deaths would be from fallout in the midwestern states that contain ICBM complexes (Montana, Wyoming, North Dakota, South

Dakota, Missouri, Arkansas, Kansas, and Arizona) and in the states immediately downwind.

12. Do we maintain some bombers in the air at all times?

Answer: No, although we once did. In the early 1960s we kept a few dozen B-52 bombers in the air at all times. These bombers would fly north to positions in the Arctic, remain in a holding pattern for a few hours, and then return to their bases. This practice was halted in the mid-1960s, primarily because of the expense. Because of our sophisticated satellite warning systems, we are confident that we can get most of our bombers off the ground even if the Soviets launch a "bolt from the blue" attack.

13. Would the U.S. intercontinental bombers return to the United States after delivering their nuclear weapons against the Soviet Union?

Answer: No—with a possible few exceptions. U.S. bombers are refueled by KC-135 tankers in midair on their way to the Soviet Union. After they have launched their missiles and dropped their bombs, they go to friendly airfields (called recovery bases) on the periphery of the Soviet Union to obtain fuel (hopefully) for the trip home. Bombers that attack targets deep in the central part of the Soviet Union would refuel at recovery bases in places like Turkey.

14. How accurate are ballistic missiles?

Answer: Current U.S. ICBMs have accuracies of about 600–1,000 feet. Current Soviet ICBMs have accuracies of about 1,000–1,500 feet. Future ICBMs which use satellites to correct their trajectories could be accurate to within a few hundred feet.

Current SLBMs are not as accurate as ICBMs— about 1,500 feet for U.S. SLBMs and 3,000 feet for Soviet SLBMs.

The 1,000-mile Pershing II missile which we plan to deploy in Europe beginning in 1983 uses a special radar-assisted guidance system to obtain accuracies of less than 100 feet. To obtain these high accuracies, a radar in the nose of the missile scans the terrain as the missile descends towards its target. The guidance system then matches the resulting radar map with a computer-stored map and makes the necessary course corrections. A similar technique might someday be used to achieve accuracies of 50 to 100 feet for ICBMs and SLBMs.

The technical term for the accuracies cited above is Circular Error Probable (CEP). The term simply refers to the radius of a circle within which half the missile warheads will fall. Thus if a particular type of missile is said to have an accuracy (or a CEP) of 1,000 feet, half the warheads from missiles of this type will fall within 1,000 feet of their targets and half will fall at distances greater than 1,000 feet.

15. How accurate are cruise missiles?

Answer: Current U.S. cruise missiles (such as those being deployed on B-52 bombers and those slated for deployment in Europe beginning in 1983) have accuracies of about 300 feet. Current Soviet cruise missiles (which are all of very old design) have accuracies of about one mile against land targets. Some Soviet cruise missiles are designed for use against ships and have homing devices which give them antiship accuracies of about 50 feet. U.S. cruise missiles currently use a guidance system called TERCOM (Terrain Contour Matching) which employs a radar altimeter to match the altitude contour of the ground with an on-board map obtained from satellite photos. The potential accuracy for such a system is about 100 feet, with the last map-matching update about 20 to 30 miles from the target. If a television camera could be mounted on the missile, a more sophisticated "scene-matching" system could in principle improve cruise missile accuracy to about 20 to 30 *feet*.

16. If terrorists were able to steal a nuclear weapon from a U.S. storage site, would they be able to set it off?

Answer: Almost certainly not. Almost all U.S. nuclear weapons contain a series of so-called Permissive Action Links (PALs) which make them tamperproof. Any effort to get inside the weapon would immediately disable it. However, a clever technician could probably reclaim the nuclear material in the weapon.

17. What is the smallest nuclear weapon in the U.S. inventory?

Answer: We have some battlefield nuclear weapons which are of a "dial-a-yield" character. This means that the yield can be preset by a battlefield commander to any of several values between, for example, one half a kiloton and one hundred kilotons. The low-yield options on these weapons constitute our lowest-yield nuclear weapons.

18. How much damage could Chinese missile forces do to the Soviet Union? To the United States?

Answer: At present, the Chinese medium- and intermediate-range ballistic missile force of about a hundred single-warhead land-based missiles (a few megatons apiece) could probably destroy the top forty cities in the Soviet Union in a first strike. Soviet fatalities would be about thirty million people. If the Soviet Union attacked the Chinese first, it is not clear how many Chinese missiles would survive, but it could be as high as ten to twenty—adequate to destroy Moscow and several other major Soviet cities in a retaliatory attack.

The Chinese have been testing an 8,000-mile ICBM (the CSS-4) capable of reaching targets in the United States, but the missile is either not yet deployed or deployed in only a few silos. Two such ICBMs targeted against the two largest cities in the United States (New York and Los Angeles) would kill about ten million people.

19. How much damage could French and British nuclear forces do to the Soviet Union?

Answer: The French nuclear force of eighty submarine-launched ballistic missiles (SLBMs), eighteen land-based missiles, and twenty-four medium bombers could probably destroy the thirty largest Soviet cities (twenty-five million people) in a first strike. If the Soviet Union attacked the French first, few if any of the land-based missiles and bombers would survive, but all French submarines at sea would probably survive. Thus, if two or three of the five submarines (64–80 SLBMs) were at sea, a retaliatory attack by the French could probably destroy the top fifteen to twenty Soviet cities (fifteen to twenty million people).

The British nuclear force of sixty-four SLBMs and forty medium bombers has about the same capability as the French—destruction of thirty Soviet cities in a first strike and fifteen to twenty Soviet cities in a retaliatory strike.

20. How long will it take before China has a missile force as large as that currently possessed by the United States and the Soviet Union?

Answer: The present Chinese medium- and intermediate-range missile force of about one hundred missiles is not growing very fast—only a few missiles per year. The Chinese currently have no SLBMs. Since China cannot begin to match U.S. and Soviet missile production capability, it will probably be at least twenty and maybe thirty or forty years before the Chinese have as many ICBMs and SLBMs as the United States (1,700) or the Soviet Union (2,350) currently possesses.

APPENDIX B

Glossary of Nuclear War Terms

ABM Treaty: One of the two agreements signed at Moscow on May 26, 1972, known collectively as the SALT I agreements. The ABM Treaty was ratified by the U.S. Senate by a vote of 88–2 and entered into force on October 3, 1972. The treaty is of unlimited duration. The original ABM Treaty limited each side to two ABM deployment areas (one national capital area and one ICBM silo launcher area) with restrictions on the deployment of ABM launchers and interceptors (one hundred of each per area) and ABM radars at these areas. A protocol to the treaty signed in 1974 further restricted each side to only one ABM deployment area.

Aggregate: A term used in SALT and discussions of the strategic balance. It refers to the total number of ICBM launchers, SLBM launchers, and intercontinental bombers on a side.

Air-Launched Cruise Missile (ALCM): A cruise missile designed to be launched from an aircraft.

Air-to-Surface Ballistic Missile (ASBM): A ballistic missile launched from an airplane against a target on the earth's surface. Neither side currently has such missiles.

Alpha Particle: A positively charged particle emitted by certain radioactive materials. Alpha particles can be stopped by a sheet of paper.

Antiballistic Missile (ABM) System: The interceptor missiles, radars, and associated equipment of a system designed to intercept and destroy enemy ballistic missiles.

Antisubmarine Warfare (ASW): Operations conducted with the intention of destroying or rendering ineffective enemy submarines.

Assured Destruction: The ability to inflict a very high level of damage on enemy population centers, industry, military forces, and other resources even after absorbing a surprise first strike by enemy nuclear forces. *See* Mutual Assured Destruction.

Atom: The basic component of all matter; the smallest part of an element that has all the chemical properties of that element. Atoms are in turn made up of protons, neutrons, and electrons.

Attack Submarine: A submarine designed to destroy enemy naval vessels and merchant shipping.

Backfire: The NATO designation for a type of modern Soviet supersonic bomber. It is currently being deployed to operational units for use in a theater or naval strike role as a replacement for older Soviet medium bombers. Backfire has characteristics which fall between the characteristics of existing intercontinental or medium bombers used for naval and other peripheral attack missions.

Background Radiation: The radioactivity in the environment, including cosmic rays from space and radiation that exists everywhere—in the air, in the earth, and in man-made materials that surround us. In the United States, most people receive 100 to 250 millirems of background radiation per year.

Ballistic Missile: A missile that consists of a rocket booster and a payload (one or more warheads), where the missile follows an archlike flight path (like the St. Louis arch) to its target. The rocket booster operates for about the first 10 to 15 percent of the time the missile is in flight. After the desired velocity and flight direction have been achieved, the rocket booster shuts off and usually separates from the payload. Thereafter, the payload continues on the arched flight path and is acted upon predominantly by gravity—which is the meaning of the term *ballistic*.

Booster: That portion of a missile which contains the rocket engines and the fuel. In a single-warhead missile, the guidance system is also part of the booster.

Broken Arrow: The Defense Department code name for an accident involving nuclear weapons—the crash of an aircraft carrying nuclear weapons, for example.

Chain Reaction: a self-sustaining series of events occurring when a neutron splits an atom, releasing a sufficient number of neutrons to cause many other atoms to split in the same way.

Circular Error Probable (CEP): A measure of the delivery accuracy of a weapon system. It is the radius of a circle around a target, of such size that a weapon aimed at the target has a 50 percent probability of falling within the circle.

Civil Defense: Protection of the general population, leadership, and industry from nuclear attack.

Command and Control: The facilities, equipment, and personnel that acquire, process and disseminate information needed by decision makers in directing and controlling military operations.

Counterforce Capability: Literally, the ability to destroy enemy military forces. However, the term is most often used to refer to the ability to destroy enemy ICBM silos.

Countervalue Attack: The employment of military forces to destroy nonmilitary targets—population centers, industry, resources, etc.

Critical Mass: The smallest amount of fissionable material capable of sustaining a chain reaction.

Cruise Missile: A pilotless jet airplane—or, in technical terms, a guided missile that uses aerodynamic lift to offset gravity and uses propulsion to counteract drag. A cruise missile's flight path remains within the earth's atmosphere, and its engine burns throughout its flight.

Cruise Missile Carrier (CMC): An aircraft equipped for launching a cruise missile. The term is often used to refer to a possible future U.S. military aircraft (e.g., a modified 747) which would carry dozens of cruise missiles.

Damage Limitation: Any efforts, active or passive, to limit damage from nuclear strikes. ABM systems, air defense systems, and civil defense are all "damage limitation" techniques.

Deterrence: A strategy or situation in which enemy leaders are convinced that aggression is an unattractive alternative because the potential losses (and risk of escalation) offset anticipated gains.

Deuterium: A form of hydrogen in which the nucleus contains a proton and a neutron rather than simply a proton. Deuterium is part of the fuel in a fusion reaction. Deuterium occurs naturally in the oceans in the form of heavy water.

Development: The first stage in the process of producing a weapon system. Subsequent stages include testing (or flight-testing), production, and deployment.

Dynamic Pressure: The force created by wind. For example, a sailboat moves because of the dynamic pressure of the wind.

Electron: A subatomic particle with a negative electrical charge and a mass 1/1837 that of a proton. When electrons are emitted by radioactive material, they are often referred to as *beta particles*. A beta particle can be stopped by an inch of wood or a thick sheet of aluminum.

Encryption: Encoding communications for the purpose of concealing information. In SALT, this term was applied to a practice whereby a side alters the manner in which it transmits telemetry from a weapon being tested, rendering the information undecipherable.

Enriched Fuel: Uranium that has been modified by increasing the concentration of the fissionable isotope uranium 235. Enriched fuel is more able to sustain a chain reaction and is normally used as the fuel for a nuclear power plant.

Escalation: An increase (deliberate or unpremeditated) in the scope or intensity of a conflict.

Fallout: The radioactive particles that are carried into the upper atmosphere by a nuclear explosion and fall to earth downwind from the explosion, often in rain.

Fallout Shelter: A shelter covered by a material such as dirt or concrete which protects the occupants from the radioactivity in fallout. An effective fallout shelter requires some means of removing particles from the air taken into the shelter.

Fireball: The very hot (10,000,000°F.) central region of a nuclear explosion.

First Strike: Literally, the first offensive move of a war. The term is frequently used to refer to a major nuclear attack on enemy nuclear forces such as ICBM silos, bomber bases, etc. Also called *preemptive strike.*

Fission: The splitting or breaking apart of a heavy atom into two new atoms. When a heavy atom, such as uranium, is split, large amounts of energy and two or three neutrons are usually released.

Fission Products: The atoms formed when uranium or plutonium is split in a nuclear reaction. Fission products are usually radioactive.

Flexible Response: A strategy for controlling escalation whereby an escalation by the enemy in the level of conflict is met with a measured response designed to limit the conflict to the degree possible.

Flight Test: For a missile, the actual launch of that missile conducted for any purpose, including the development of the missile, the demonstration of its capabilities, and the training of crews.

Fractional Orbital Bombardment System (FOBS): A missile that achieves an orbital trajectory around the earth (e.g., at a 100-mile altitude) but fires a set of retro-rockets before the completion of one revolution in order to slow down, reenter the atmosphere, and release the warhead it carries into a ballistic trajectory toward its target.

Fractionation: The division of the payload of a missile into several warheads. The use of a MIRV payload is an example of fractionation.

Fusion: The fusing, or joining together, of two atomic nuclei in a reaction which releases large amounts of energy and one or more neutrons.

Gamma Rays: A form of high energy electromagnetic radiation emitted from a nucleus. Gamma rays are essentially the same as X rays and require heavy shielding, such as lead brick, to stop them.

General War: Armed conflict between the United States, the Soviet Union, and their respective allies, in which the total military resources of the two sides, including nuclear weapons, are employed. Also known as *general nuclear war* or *all-out nuclear war.*

Ground-Launched Cruise Missile (GLCM): A cruise missile launched from ground installations or vehicles.

Ground Zero: The point on the earth's surface (i.e., the geographical coordinates) at which a nuclear weapon is detonated. For an airburst, it is the point on the earth's surface directly below the point of detonation.

Guidance System: That part of the missile which contains the computer and other devices which guide a ballistic missile to the proper velocity and direction for booster (or postboost vehicle) thrust cutoff. In the case of cruise missiles, the guidance system takes the missile all the way to its target.

Half-Life: The length of time in which any radioactive substance will lose one half of its radioactivity. The half-life of a substance may vary in length from a fraction of a second to many thousands of years.

Hard Target: A target protected against the blast and associated effects of nuclear weapons through structural hardening. An underground concrete-reinforced ICBM silo is an example of a hard target.

Heavy Bomber: A term used in the SALT negotiations to distinguish the principal intercontinental bombers on the two sides (the B-52 and B-1 for the United States and the Bear and Bison for the Soviet Union) from other bombers.

Heavy Missile: A term used in the SALT negotiations where ballistic missiles were divided into two categories—light and heavy—according to their size and payload.

Heavy Water: Water in which the hydrogen atoms contain an extra neutron. These atoms are called deuterium.

Implosion: The inverse of an explosion. In an explosion, material travels away from a central point; in an implosion, material travels toward a central point. Essentially, nuclear weapons employ an implosion to concentrate and hold a critical mass of fissionable material.

Infrared Detectors: Devices that operate at infrared wavelengths and detect objects because of their temperature. Higher temperature objects are said to have larger *infrared signatures*.

Intercontinental Ballistic Missile (IBM): A ballistic missile capable of reaching targets at intercontinental distances—normally defined as a range in excess of 5,500 kilometers.

Intermediate-Range Ballistic Missile (IRBM): A ballistic missile with a range of between 2,200 and 5,500 kilometers.

International Atomic Energy Agency (IAEA): The agency that monitors activities at nuclear power plants and other nuclear-related activities to help inhibit the proliferation of nuclear weapons.

Isotopes: Different forms of the same chemical element which are distinguished by having different numbers of neutrons in the nucleus. A single element may have many isotopes. For example, there are three isotopes of hydrogen.

Kamikaze: The World War II Japanese pilots who tried, sometimes successfully, to crash airplanes into U.S. Navy ships in order to sink them.

Kiloton: A thousand tons of TNT—a measure of the explosive power of nuclear weapons. One thousand kilotons equals one megaton.

Laser: A device which produces an intense beam of light entirely of the same wavelength.

Launch on Warning: The policy or strategy of launching ICBMs on the basis of information supplied by satellite and other warning systems which indicate that an enemy missile attack is coming. Also known as *Launch under Attack.*

Laydown: The process of matching nuclear weapons against targets on the other side.

Limited Nuclear War: A nuclear war that involves the use of a limited number (e.g., a few dozen or a few hundred) nuclear weapons. *See* General War.

Limited Test Ban Treaty (LTBT): A treaty signed in 1963 which prohibits the signatory nations from conducting nuclear weapons tests in the atmosphere, underwater, or in space. Underground tests are permitted.

Liquid-Fueled Missile: A missile in which the fuel is liquid. The fuel usually consists of two chemicals which react when brought together in a high-temperature combustion chamber.

Megaton: A million tons of TNT—a measure of the explosive power of nuclear weapons.

Military-Industrial Complex: The term coined by President Eisenhower to describe the combined interests of the military and the defense industry in obtaining new weapons systems.

Multiple Independently Targetable Reentry Vehicle (MIRV): Multiple reentry vehicles carried by a ballistic missile, each of which can be directed to a separate and arbitrarily located target. A MIRV missile employs a postboost vehicle (PBV) or other warhead-dispensing mechanism.

Multiple Reentry Vehicle (MRV): The reentry vehicle of a ballistic missile equipped with multiple warheads, where the missile does not have the capability of independently targeting the reentry vehicles—as distinct from a missile equipped for MIRVs.

Mutual Assured Destruction: The strategy of preventing nuclear war whereby each side maintains an assured destruction capability. *See* Assured Destruction.

National Technical Means of Verification (NTM): A SALT term which refers to the assets that a nation uses for verifying compliance with the provisions of an arms control agreement. NTM include photographic reconnaissance satellites and aircraft-based systems (such as radars), as well as sea- and ground-based systems (such as radars and antennae for collecting telemetry).

Neutron: A subatomic particle with no electrical charge and a mass equal to that of a proton.

Nonproliferation Treaty (NPT): A treaty first signed in 1968 in which the signatory nations that do not have nuclear weapons agree to forgo them while the signatory nations that do have nuclear weapons agree to work to prevent proliferation and assist in the development of peaceful uses of nuclear energy.

Nuclear Weapon: A nuclear bomb or warhead.

Nuclear Weapon Delivery System: Any means (missile, bomber, etc.) by which a nuclear weapon is delivered to a target.

Overpressure: The amount by which the pressure of a shock wave or blast wave exceeds the normal sea-level atmospheric pressure of 14.7 pounds per square inch.

Particle Beam Weapon: A device for producing an intense beam of subatomic particles, usually electrons.

Payload: The weapons and penetration aids carried by a nuclear weapons delivery vehicle (bomber or missile).

Penetration Aids (Penaids): Devices employed by offensive weapon systems, such as ballistic missiles and bombers, to increase the probability of penetrating enemy defenses. They are frequently designed to simulate or to mask an aircraft or ballistic missile warhead in order to mislead enemy radar and/or divert defensive antiaircraft or anti-missile fire.

Postboost Vehicle (PBV): Often referred to as a *bus*, the postboost vehicle (PBV) is that part of a MIRVed missile which carries the warheads, a guidance package, fuel, and small rockets for altering the ballistic flight path so that the warheads can be dispensed sequentially toward different targets.

Preemptive Strike: See First Strike.

Production: Series manufacturing of a particular strategic nuclear delivery system following its development and testing.

Proliferation: The process by which one nation after another comes into possession of nuclear weapons.

Proton: A subatomic particle with a positive electrical charge and a mass 1,837 times that of an electron.

Radar: A device which transmits and receives electromagnetic signals of radio wavelengths as a means of detecting missiles or aircraft. Large objects that reflect radio waves efficiently are said to have a large *radar cross section*.

Radiation: Energy in the form of gamma rays or particles which are emitted by disintegrating atoms.

Radioactivity: The property possessed by some elements, such as uranium, of spontaneously emitting alpha, beta, or gamma rays.

Reentry Vehicle (RV): That portion of a ballistic missile which carries the nuclear warhead. It is called a reentry vehicle because it reenters the earth's atmosphere in the terminal portion of the missile trajectory.

Rem: An acronym for *Roentgen Equivalent Man*, a measure of radiation exposure which indicates the potential impact on human cells.

Retaliatory Strike: An attack on an enemy that has initiated hostilities with a first strike. Sometimes called *second strike*.

Second Strike: See Retaliatory Strike.

Short-Range Attack Missile (SRAM): A missile with a range of about 100 kilometers and a warhead yield of 200 kilotons, carried on a U.S. bomber.

Shroud: The metal shield that covers a MIRV payload and protects the warheads and the postboost vehicle during the boost phase of the flight.

Silo Launcher: A "hard" fixed underground ballistic missile launcher, usually of steel and concrete, housing an intercontinental ballistic missile and the equipment for launching it.

Soft Target: A target not protected against blast or the associated effects of nuclear weapons.

Solid-Fueled Missile: A missile in which the fuel is solid. The fuel usually consists of two chemicals which burn under control once they are ignited, much like a Fourth of July sparkler.

Spent Fuel: Nuclear fuel, containing fission products, that can no longer economically sustain a chain reaction.

Spheres of Influence: The geographical regions dominated respectively by the United States (the Western Hemisphere) and the Soviet Union (Eastern Europe).

SSBN: The U.S. Navy term for a nuclear-powered ballistic missile submarine.

Strategic Arms Limitation Talks (SALT): A series of negotiations between the United States and the Soviet Union which began in November of 1969. The negotiations seek to limit and reduce both offensive and defensive strategic arms. The first round of negotiations, known as SALT I, concluded in May 1972, resulting in two agreements: the ABM Treaty and an Interim Agreement on offensive arms. SALT II, signed in June of 1979 but not ratified by the U.S. Senate, is a comprehensive treaty limiting strategic offensive weapons.

Strategic Nuclear Weapons: A term which generally refers to long-range nuclear weapons delivery vehicles, such as ICBMs, SLBMs, and intercontinental bombers.

Submarine-Launched Ballistic Missile (SLBM): A ballistic missile carried in and launched from a submarine.

Submarine-Launched Cruise Missile (SLCM): A cruise missile launched from a submarine.

Superpowers: The United States and the Soviet Union.

Supersonic: Exceeding the speed of sound, which at ground level is about 740 miles per hour.

Tactical Nuclear Weapons: A term which generally refers to nuclear weapons used on the battlefield or in other limited nuclear war situations. For example, U.S. nuclear weapons in Europe and on aircraft carriers are called *tactical nuclear weapons*.

Telemetry: The data transmitted by radio to the personnel conducting a missile test, which are used to monitor the functions and performance of the missile during the course of the test.

Theater Nuclear Forces (TNF): Those nuclear forces deployed in a particular "theater," such as the European theater or the Pacific theater. The term *long-range theater nuclear forces* refers to medium-range missiles and bombers deployed in a particular theater.

Thermal Radiation: The "heat" given off by a nuclear explosion.

Thermonuclear Weapons: Nuclear weapons in which fusion reactions take place. The term reflects the requirement for achieving very high temperatures—several million degrees—before the fusion reaction takes place.

Throw-Weight: Ballistic missile throw-weight is the useful weight that is placed on a trajectory toward the target by the boost stages of the missile. For a single-warhead missile, it consists of the weight of the warhead. For a MIRVed missile, it consists of the weight of the warheads plus the weight of the postboost vehicle.

Triad: The combination of ICBMs, SLBMs, and intercontinental bombers, each of which presents different defensive problems to an enemy.

Tritium: A form of hydrogen in which the nucleus contains a proton and two neutrons rather than simply a single proton. Tritium is part of the fuel in a fusion reaction. Tritium does not occur naturally but, like plutonium, can be produced in nuclear reactors.

Verification: The process of determining, to the extent necessary to adequately safeguard national security, that the other side is complying with an arms-control agreement. This process of judging adequacy takes into account the monitoring capabilities of existing and future intelligence-collection systems and analysis techniques as well as the ability of the other side to evade detection if it should attempt to do so.

War-Fighting Strategy: A strategy in which forces are designed to fight any kind of war at any level of conflict.

Warhead: That part of a missile or other munition which contains the nuclear or other explosive system.

Worst Case: In estimates of future enemy military capabilities, the most extreme situation imaginable.

Yellowcake: A uranium compound which occurs in the uranium ore refining process.

Yield: The energy released in a nuclear explosion. The energy released in the detonation of a nuclear weapon is generally measured in terms of the kilotons (KT) or megatons (MT) of TNT required to produce the same energy release.

APPENDIX C
The Arms Race in Numbers

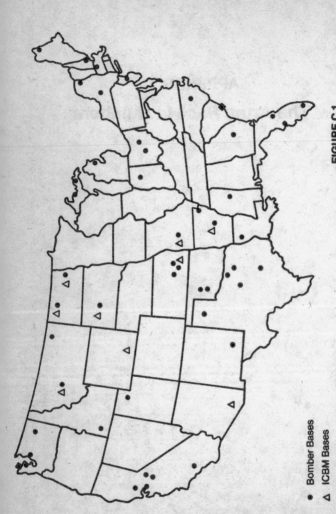

• Bomber Bases
△ ICBM Bases
■ Ballistic Missile Submarine Bases

FIGURE C.1
Location of U.S. Missile and Bomber Bases

TABLE C.1
The U.S.-Soviet Strategic Arms Race

	ICBMs		SLBMs		Bombers		Total Strategic Delivery Vehicles		Total Warheads		Total Megatons*	
	US	USSR	US	USSR	US	USSR	US	USSR	US	USSR	US	USSR
1990**	1,350	1,700	720	1,300	450	200	2,550	3,200	18,000	20,000	7,100	13,000
1985***	1,052	1,500	664	1,100	348	140	2,064	2,740	13,300	10,000	4,200	9,200
1982	1,052	1,400	632	950	348	140	2,032	2,490	11,000	8,000	4,100	7,100
1980	1,054	1,400	640	950	348	140	2,042	2,490	10,000	6,000	4,000	5,700
1978	1,054	1,400	656	810	348	140	2,058	2,350	9,800	5,200	3,800	5,400
1976	1,054	1,500	656	750	390	140	2,100	2,390	9,400	3,200	3,700	4,500
1974	1,054	1,600	656	640	470	140	2,180	2,380	8,400	2,400	3,800	4,200
1972	1,054	1,500	656	450	520	140	2,230	2,090	5,800	2,100	4,100	4,000
1970	1,054	1,300	656	240	520	140	2,230	1,680	3,900	1,800	4,300	3,100
1968	1,054	850	656	40	650	155	2,360	1,045	4,500	850	5,100	2,300
1966	1,054	250	592	30	750	155	2,396	435	5,000	550	5,600	1,200
1964	800	200	336	20	1,280	155	2,416	375	6,800	500	7,500	1,000
1962	80	40	144	20	1,650	155	1,874	290	7,400	400	8,000	800
1960	20	a few	32	15	1,650	130	1,702	150	6,500	300	7,200	600

*The figures shown are for "equivalent megatons," the most commonly used measure of aggregate explosive power. It is obtained by taking the square root of weapon yields above one megaton and the cube root of weapon yields below one megaton.

**Assumes no SALT Treaty limiting strategic offensive weapons. The numbers shown are extrapolations of official U.S. estimates provided in congressional testimony on the SALT II Treaty.

TABLE C.2
U.S. Missiles and Bombers

ICBMs	Date First Operational	Max. Number Deployed	Number Now Deployed	Number of Warheads	Est. Yield per Warhead
Atlas	1960	108	0	1	2–5MT
Titan I	1962	54	0	1	5MT
Titan II	1963	54	52	1	9MT
Minuteman I	1963	800	0	1	1MT
Minuteman II	1966	500	450	1	1MT
Minuteman III	1970	550	550	3	170–350KT
M-X	1986(?)	—	—	10–12	350KT
SLBMs					
Polaris A1	1960	80	0	1	1MT
Polaris A2	1962	208	0	1	1MT
Polaris A3	1965	400	112	1	1MT
Poseidon	1971	496	352	6–14	40KT
Trident I	1980	168	168	8	100KT
Trident II	19??	—	—	8	350KT

Bombers

B-47	1950	1500	0	4	1MT
B-52 (A–F)	1955	450	90	4	1MT
B-52 (G–H)	1962	290	260	12–20	200KT/1MT
B-58	1962	70	0	5	1MT
B-1	1984(?)	—	—	12–20	200KT/1MT

TABLE C.3
Soviet Missiles and Bombers

ICBMs	Date First Operational	Max. Number Deployed	Number Now Deployed	Number of Warheads	Est. Yield per Warhead
SS-6	1960	4	0	1	4MT
SS-7	1962	200	0	1	4MT
SS-8	1963	25	0	1	4MT
SS-9	1967	288	0	1	25MT
SS-11	1966	970	520	1	1MT
SS-13	1969	60	60	1	1MT
SS-X-16	—	0	0	3	200KT
SS-17	1975	150	150	4	about 700 KT
SS-18	1974	308	308	10	about 1 MT
SS-19	1975	360	360	6	about 700 KT
SLBMs					
SS-N-4	1960	15	0	1	1MT
SS-N-5	1964	24	0	1	1MT
SS-N-6	1968	496	416	1	1MT

SS-N-8	1973	280	280	1	2MT
SS-N-18	1978	176	176	6	200KT
Typhoon	1983(?)	—	—	6–8	?
Bombers					
Bison	1956	70	35	2	5MT
Bear	1956	110	105	1–3	5MT
Backfire	1975	300	300	1–4	?
Tu-160	198?	—	—	—	—

TABLE C.4
Nuclear Forces of Great Britain, France, and China

	Great Britain	France	China
ICBMs	0	0	a few
MRBMs and IRBMs	0	18	about 100
SLBMs	64	80	0
Medium Bombers*	60	40	about 100

*The British bombers (Vulcans) and the French bombers (Mirage IVs) can reach targets in the western part of the Soviet Union. The Chinese bombers (Badgers) can reach targets throughout the Soviet Union.